# POWER NEGOTIATING
Strategies for
Winning in
Life and Business

# POWER NEGOTIATING
## Strategies for Winning in Life and Business

JOHN ILICH

PHILLIPS MEMORIAL
LIBRARY
PROVIDENCE COLLEGE

Addison-Wesley Publishing Company
Reading, Massachusetts
Menlo Park, California • London • Amsterdam • Don Mills, Ontario • Sydney

BF
637
N4
I45

---

**Library of Congress Cataloging in Publication Data**

Ilich, John, 1933-
  Power negotiating.

  1. Negotiation.  2. Power (Social science)
3. Business.  I. Title.
HF5353.I43   650'.1     79-12646
ISBN 0-201-03149-3

---

Copyright © 1980 by Addison-Wesley Publishing Company, Inc. Philippines copyright 1980 by Addison-Wesley Publishing Company, Inc.

All rights reserved. No part of this publication may be reproduced, stored in a retrieval system, or transmitted, in any form or by any means, electronic, mechanical, photocopying, recording, or otherwise, without the prior written permission of the publisher. Printed in the United States of America. Published simultaneously in Canada. Library of Congress Catalog Card No. 79-12646.

ISBN 0-201-03149-3
ABCDEFGHIJ-AL-79

*There are but two powers in the world, the sword and the mind. In the long run the sword is always beaten by the mind.*

Napoleon

# How This Book Will Help Make You a More Powerful Negotiator

Whether you are a professional negotiator as I am or need to increase your negotiating skill in order to become more effective in dealing with situations such as purchasing or remodeling a home, purchasing an automobile or an appliance, or even asking the boss for that well-deserved raise, understanding and using negotiating power will materially enhance your chances of success.

This book covers in detail the use of power in negotiation. It explains what negotiating power is and tells and demonstrates how and when negotiating power can and should be used in order to help you become a more powerful negotiator in any negotiating situation.

It is highly important to possess a working arsenal of power negotiating techniques. The power techniques contained in this book have been tried and tested in countless negotiations, many of which involved millions of dollars. All of the techniques are explained and illustrated in a practical and useful manner for ease in application in virtually any type of negotiation, irrespective of the amount of dollars involved or the number of parties to the negotiation.

Explained in detail is the importance of your possessing a precise knowledge of the conception of power. In addition, clearly set forth is the relationship of leverage to negotiating power and how "exact" amounts of leverage should be used in each negotiating situation in order to exert the greatest amount of negotiating power.

x    How This Book Will Help Make You a More Powerful Negotiator

An essential element in virtually any negotiation is the ability to discover, sometimes instantly during the heat of negotiation, precisely how your negotiating opponent is attempting to use negotiating power against you. This book sets forth in detail how to make such discoveries, both prior to and during the negotiation, and what to do about them in order to substantially increase your chances of attaining negotiation success.

Use of power in negotiation can sometimes be the art of persuasion at its subtlest. At these times, your negotiating opponents never fully realize that they are being "persuaded." At other times, negotiating power can be the art of persuasion at its bluntest.

For purposes of clarity the terms "negotiator" and "opponent" are used throughout the text.

Finally, women are now in the forefront of our society, a very welcome and refreshing development. With this emergence, of course, comes the necessity for women to sharpen their negotiating skills. Knowledge and application of the material in this book will materially assist them in attaining that important goal.

*Grand Rapids, Michigan*  J.I.
*November 1979*

# Contents

| | | |
|---|---|---|
| 1 | Power Negotiating Defined | 1 |
| 2 | An Essential Preliminary Step to Using Negotiating Power | 5 |
| 3 | The Importance of Understanding and Using Leverage to Increase Negotiating Power | 11 |
| 4 | Why an Accurate Conception of Power Is Essential to Consistent Negotiation Success | 15 |
| 5 | Facts Are the Foundation on Which to Build Solid Negotiating Power | 25 |
| 6 | Power Techniques—The Instruments of Negotiating Power | 29 |
| 7 | The "Rainy Day" Power Negotiating Technique | 33 |
| 8 | The "Exhausting" Power Negotiating Technique | 39 |
| 9 | The "Paper Stack" Power Negotiating Technique | 43 |
| 10 | The "War and Peace" Power Negotiating Technique | 47 |
| 11 | The "Building Block" Power Negotiating Technique | 51 |

| | | |
|---|---|---|
| 12 | The "Vinegar and Honey" Power Negotiating Technique | 53 |
| 13 | The "Conduit" Power Negotiating Technique | 57 |
| 14 | The "Silence" Power Negotiating Technique | 61 |
| 15 | The "Timely Disclosure" Power Negotiating Technique | 65 |
| 16 | The "You-Say-You-Don't-But-You-Do" Power Negotiating Technique | 69 |
| 17 | The "Gearshifting" Power Negotiating Technique | 73 |
| 18 | The "Self-Depreciating" Power Negotiating Technique | 77 |
| 19 | The "It's-a-Shame-to" Power Negotiating Technique | 81 |
| 20 | Fear—The Emotional Trigger of Motivation | 85 |
| 21 | The Negotiator's Language as a Source of Negotiating Power | 91 |
| | The negotiator's language should get the opponent's attention | 92 |
| | How it is said is as important as what is said | 93 |
| | The negotiator's language should enthuse—not confuse | 94 |
| | The negotiator's language is the vehicle of negotiating power | 96 |

|    | The negotiator's language should fit the circumstances of the negotiation | 97 |
|----|---|---|
|    | The negotiator should avoid words that tend to polarize the opponent's thinking | 98 |
|    | The language used need not follow formal grammatical rules | 99 |
|    | The negotiator's language should be sincere | 100 |
|    | Reaping the benefits of the "power of the pen" is essential to consistent negotiation success | 101 |
| 22 | The Step Method of Using Negotiating Power | 105 |
| 23 | How Mental Practice Increases Negotiating Power | 109 |
| 24 | Motivating an Opponent through Your Facial Expressions | 113 |
| 25 | Making Assumptions to Increase Negotiating Power | 117 |
| 26 | Nonverbal Forms of Negotiating Power | 123 |
|    | The negotiator's charisma as a source of negotiating power | 124 |
|    | The role of titles and labels in negotiating power | 126 |
|    | The power of the negotiator's appearance | 130 |

|    | Reputation as a source of negotiating power | 132 |
|----|---|---|
|    | Organizational memberships as a source of negotiating power | 134 |
| 27 | Why It Is Necessary to Avoid Large, Initial Concessions | 135 |
| 28 | How Negotiating Obstacles and Difficulties Can Increase Negotiating Power | 139 |
| 29 | Avoiding Loss of Negotiating Power by Insulating Oneself from Snap, Often Regrettable, Decisions | 143 |
| 30 | How to Deal with Negotiating Mistakes to Minimize Loss of Negotiating Power | 147 |
| 31 | Maintaining Open Options Increases Negotiating Power | 151 |
| 32 | Delegation Can Lessen Negotiating Power | 155 |
| 33 | How Proper Habits Conserve Negotiating Power | 159 |
| 34 | The Necessity to Avoid Succumbing to Negotiating Pressures | 163 |
| 35 | Abuse of Negotiating Power | 167 |

# CHAPTER 1

# Power Negotiating Defined

*... any systematic treatment of a subject should begin with a definition so that everyone may understand what is the object of the inquiry.*

Cicero

The word "power" means, literally, the ability to accomplish objectives. Often power is equated with physical strength, force, or high position. The United States Armed Forces are considered powerful by virtue of their numbers, armaments, and sheer capability. The President of the United States is considered a person who possesses great power because of his position as leader of the strongest nation in the world. In fact, the President is often referred to as the "most powerful person in the world."

In negotiation, physical strength or force is normally not a factor (except when nations are involved), and most frequently the negotiating parties do not possess a high position from which they could derive their negotiating power. If they did possess such a position, of course, their position could become a source of negotiating power and, as will be later illustrated, could be used to influence the outcome of the negotiation.

If, then, the literal definition of power is the ability to accomplish objectives, it is equally important to bear in mind that in order to accomplish objectives in negotiation, you must motivate others. All negotiations must, in the final analysis, involve some form of contact between two or more persons. It is, therefore, clear that the definition of power negotiating is concerned essentially with your ability to motivate others.

Power negotiating, hence, can be defined as: *The ability of the negotiator to motivate an opponent in a manner that is favorable to the negotiator's negotiating objectives.* The key words are "motivate" and "favorable to the negotiator's negotiating objectives." A motivated person is one that is acting—but one that must be acting in a manner favorable to the negotiator's negotiating objectives.

### The "Crooked Picture" Power Negotiating Technique

Several years ago I was on the program of a negotiation seminar at which one of the speakers advocated that the physical environment in which negotiations were held should *always* be kept as neat as a pin. In particular, the pictures on the wall should be hanging straight so that they would not distract an opponent from concentrating on what the negotiator was saying.

It is a psychological fact that the human mind usually can concentrate on only one matter at a time, except when a matter becomes habitual. Dividing the opponent's attention between crooked pictures and concentrating on the negotiator's presentation may, indeed, adversely affect the negotiator's position. But what about a situation in which the negotiator knows or has strong reason to suspect that the opponent has the stronger of the two negotiating positions? Might it not be better in such a situation for the negotiator to have crooked pictures and other distractions such as sloppily stacked papers, books, and even overflowing ash trays? Such an environment might be effective, particularly if the opponent is a perfectionist and cannot function properly unless everything *is* in order. And if those crooked pictures and other unkempt items do, in fact, impair the opponent's concentration and effectiveness, wouldn't those items become a form of negative motivation that would be favorable to the negotiator's negotiating objectives?

The element of power in the crooked picture situation is the act of breaking the opponent's concentration and causing the opponent to not do as well as he or she could have otherwise done. The crooked pictures and other unkempt items become the instruments or mechanisms that help to break the opponent's concentration.

If the crooked pictures and other unkempt items impair the opponent's concentration on what the negotiator is saying, they clearly represent the use of power but the use is unfavorable to the negotiator's negotiating objectives. Obviously, the quickest and surest way to fail in any negotiation is to adopt a type of negotiating power that works against the negotiator.

However, when the negotiating power causes the opponent's concentration *on his or her own presentation* to be impaired, it is favorable to the negotiator's negotiating objectives because a decrease in an opponent's effectiveness automatically means an increase in the negotiator's effectiveness. If both negotiating sides possessed equal positions at the outset of the negotiation and the opponent suffers an impairment of his or her position, the negotiator's position takes on greater weight and power.

Negotiation is a very delicate business. In its purest form, it is mind pitted against mind. There is therefore a great premium placed upon concentration in the course of the discussions during which decisions with often far-reaching and significant effects must be made quickly during the heat of battle. Any distraction in such circumstances, no matter how slight, can be significant in terms of negotiating results and, in the final analysis, it is results that count. Accordingly, it is exceedingly important for the negotiator to always bear in mind, and be fully aware of, this delicate balance and of the fact that use of negotiating power is clearly a two-edged sword that can cut the negotiator as well as the opponent if not wielded prudently and with great care.

Finally, it is suggested that you reread the definition above and keep it clearly in mind while reading the rest of this text. The definition will provide you with an accurate and meaningful understanding of negotiating power and how negotiating power can be best used in virtually any negotiation that you encounter, regardless of how complex or simple or how great or small the sum involved.

CHAPTER 2

# An Essential Preliminary Step to Using Negotiating Power

*. . . our opponent is our helper.*

Edmund Burke

Before General George S. Patton, the famous World War II leader, went into combat against Field Marshal Erwin Rommel, the German "Desert Fox," he read Rommel's book on tactics using armored units, especially tanks. Through this reading Patton learned much of Rommel's thinking about armored warfare and was able to anticipate many of Rommel's moves on the battlefield. This knowledge of how his opponent's mind worked enabled Patton to defeat Rommel.

The negotiator's exercise of power in negotiation can be similarly assisted with accurate knowledge of the opponent. It is therefore important for the negotiator to learn as much as possible about his or her opponent prior to the application of any negotiating power.

### A Good Source of Knowledge—An Opponent's Habits

Hardly anywhere is there a more absolute truth than "We tell people all about ourselves by our habits." A person whose fingers are nicotine-stained is undoubtedly a heavy, habitual smoker. A person who dresses sloppily lacks self-discipline. A person who drinks coffee excessively undoubtedly is nervous or edgy because of the excessive intake of caffeine. The list is virtually endless. These outward manifestations are nothing more than a reflection of a person's habits. And it is a relatively simple process for the negotiator to arrive at an intelligent determination of an opponent's thinking based largely on observing the opponent's habits.

**Personal Contact—The Time to Be Observant!**

Frequently personal contact with the opponent does not occur until the first time the negotiator sits down with the opponent to negotiate. This is often the negotiator's earliest real opportunity to learn of the opponent's habits. It is therefore important for the negotiator to be particularly alert at this stage of the negotiation in order to be able to gain valuable knowledge about the opponent as early and as accurately as possible. This knowledge will assist the negotiator in planning and executing negotiating strategies and techniques and will increase negotiating power.

For example, I once negotiated an important matter with a man who crossed his legs every time he attempted to advocate a position that he felt was weak. I was able to equate the leg crossing activity with the advocation of weak positions by the following process. When the negotiations were under way my opponent's leg crossing became obvious at various times throughout the discussions. I therefore concluded that since the leg crossing was not constant, it must reflect how my opponent felt either about what I was advocating or he was advocating or, perhaps, a combination of both. I then eliminated myself as the cause of my opponent's leg crossing by carefully observing that he did not cross his legs no matter what positions *I* advocated. It was then a simple matter to conclude that my opponent crossed his legs whenever he advocated a position he himself considered weak. Once I discovered this, it was, of course, relatively easy to counter any positions my opponent advocated whenever he crossed his legs since I knew that he lacked confidence in those positions himself.

**Talking with Others Who Have Negotiated with the Opponent**

Attempting to learn about an opponent by conferring with others who have previously negotiated with that opponent can be productive, particularly if those approached have had considerable experience with the opponent. Using this approach, however, has several hazards that the negotiator should avoid. First, the information may be inaccurate for a variety of reasons: the person giving the information may be mistaken, biased, or prone to exaggerate.

Second, the person asked to supply the information may tell the opponent about the negotiator's request for information. If this happens, it gives the opponent the opportunity to anticipate the negotiator's moves and to even "leak" false information designed to encourage the negotiator to adopt a certain strategy or use a certain technique which the opponent can then use to his or her advantage during the negotiation. This "leaking" practice is common in negotiations of great importance, especially those between nations or large companies and unions that have access to the public media such as the press or television.

**Carefully Scrutinizing an Opponent's Written Work**

Just as Patton carefully read Rommel's book, the negotiator should, whenever the opportunity presents itself, read any of an opponent's written work or any oral statements that have found their way into print. The negotiator should pay particularly close attention to an opponent's speeches since oral declarations can be more revealing than carefully written and edited works such as books or magazine articles. Oral declarations often are made on the spur of the moment by a speaker who has not had the opportunity to rehearse, prune, or edit.

To illustrate, assume the negotiation concerns a new labor contract and the negotiator is retained to represent the labor union. The president of the company was quoted as saying "I came up the hard way without benefit of a formal education and am extremely proud of my accomplishments of building the company into its present solid financial and competitive position." The company's financial and competitive position can be accurately learned from the company's financial statements and other market information that is normally readily available from a variety of sources such as financial magazines and journals. But the president's revelation (information that may not be available elsewhere) that he "came up the hard way without the benefits of a formal education" may be useful in predicting the manner in which he may conduct himself during the negotiation. Lack of a formal education may cause him to be less familar with specific financial matters, such as wages and fringe benefits, normally involved in labor negotiations. The president may therefore have to rely heavily on financial "experts." This possibility may afford the negotiator the chance to direct the substance of his or her presentation toward those experts on all of the financial matters involved in the negotiation. If this is the case and if the opponent's financial experts concur with what the negotiator advocates, the president will be inclined to agree because of his reliance upon those experts. Of course, in spite of his background, the president *may be* quite knowledgeable about financial matters. Since the negotiator has been tipped off by the president's public statement as to the possibility that the president may lack financial knowledge, however, it is a simple matter for the negotiator to soon discover the truth by careful and tactful probing very early in the negotiation.

The fact that the president had to claw his way up the business ladder may have made him an adamant and protective person unwilling to "give away" any of the fruits of his long years of toil. Accordingly, he may very likely carry this unyielding attitude into the negotiations when the union presents its demands at the bargaining table. Anticipating this possibility, the negotiator may want to have a tentative countering strategy and prepare to provide facts and arguments to show why meeting the union's proposals will facilitate growth of the president's company and not hinder it.

**Out-of-date Writings**

Negotiators should be wary about relying too heavily on written material that may be out of date and which no longer may reflect the thinking of their opponents. Patton, in reading Rommel's work, felt confident that it reflected Rommel's current thinking because the art of desert warfare developed only during World War II. Patton, because of his enormous knowledge and background of military matters, was able to conclude with an excellent degree of certainty that he could rely upon what Rommel had written to accurately predict what Rommel would do on the battlefield.

One obvious tip that the written material may be outdated is the amount of time that has elapsed between its publication date and the date of the negotiation. Change is so rampant in today's society that even material published relatively close to the negotiation date should be checked to be certain that the chances are good that it will still reflect the opponent's thinking at the time of the negotiation. Even then, however, it is important that the negotiator probe very early in the negotiation in order to gain some tangible confirmation that the written material, indeed, still reflects the opponent's thinking.

**The Necessity for Probing**

Probing during the negotiation, especially during its early stages, is one of the best ways to obtain reliable knowledge about the opponent. You, the negotiator, should be alert from the first time your opponent comes into view, watching the opponent's actions and deducing from those actions the nature of the opponent's habits and, equally important, listening to every word the opponent says.

An opponent, for example, who smokes cigarettes down to such a short length that they virtually burn the opponent's fingers either may be financially conservative (must get every last puff out of each cigarette) or constantly preoccupied to such an extent that the cigarettes go unnoticed until they actually produce burns. An opponent who is preoccupied may not be organized well enough to skillfully carry on that particular negotiation and therefore may be vulnerable. The point is that you can materially increase your negotiating power and thus attain your negotiating objectives by watching an opponent closely, listening to what the opponent says, and applying what you see and hear toward winning the negotiation.

CHAPTER 3

# The Importance of Understanding and Using Leverage to Increase Negotiating Power

*Give me a lever long enough and a prop strong enough, I can singlehanded move the world.*

Archimedes

Leverage is the process of increasing power to attain the desired result. It is therefore important for you, in your role as negotiator, to fully understand what leverage is and how it can and should be used in negotiation.

Traditionally, the concept of leverage has been demonstrated through picturing a large, heavy object being moved by a pole. Assume the object to be moved is your opponent. In order to succeed in the negotiation, you must move your opponent favorably toward your negotiating objectives. Your tool for moving your opponent is, figuratively, a lever. It is your responsibility to create a lever long enough and strong enough to move your opponent. Indeed, the longer and stronger your lever, the greater your leverage, and the greater your leverage, the greater your power.

Applying this analogy of leverage to an actual negotiation, assume that you represent the owner of a large parcel of unimproved land that the landowner desires to sell at a top price. A prospective purchaser (your opponent) has inquired about the land. You have learned that the opponent is a large, national corporation that is looking for an expansion site and that the opponent's own survey has narrowed its choice to two sites, one of which is the land owned by your client.

Obviously, at this point your lever is much too weak and short to move the opponent to pay a top price for the land. The only real leverage that you possess is the fact that your opponent's own survey has narrowed its choice to two sites. Your opponent can still decide to purchase the other site or may be willing to buy your client's site but for a lower price than your client is seeking.

Assume that you learn that the opponent's survey concludes that your client's site is desirable for your opponent's needs because of the site's proximity to adequate utilities, labor force, living comfort, and culture for the company's plant management, including good schools for their children. You also learn that soon to be announced (and therefore probably not included in the company's survey) is the construction of a new medical facility in the area that will be one of the finest in the country. This facility will bring outstanding medical treatment to the area.

The mere possession of this knowledge does not automatically increase your negotiating leverage and thus your negotiating power. Knowledge without application is useless. You must therefore skillfully apply this knowledge in order to increase your negotiating leverage.

You know that your opponent is familiar with all of the foregoing facts (except the one concerning the construction of the new medical facility) since the facts are contained in your opponent's survey. What you must do is carefully and skillfully dwell on those facts during the negotiation so that they become dominant in your opponent's thinking. When that occurs, your opponent will be motivated toward selecting your client's site and toward your negotiating objective of selling the site for a top price. You have thus increased your negotiating leverage and thus greatly enhanced your negotiating power.

Assume that during the negotiation you dwell on all of the favorable factors in your opponent's survey but do not mention the new medical facility. You do this deliberately as part of your strategy. If you can convince your opponent based on the data contained in your opponent's survey, you will have no need to play your "ace," the fact about the construction of the new medical facility. This approach is common in negotiation. Your goal is to attain your negotiating objective and you should use your knowledge and thus increase your negotiating leverage only so far as is necessary to attain your negotiating objective. To go beyond that is to "overclose" and thus jeopardize the successful conclusion of the negotiation.

Assume, after dwelling on the data contained in your opponent's survey, that your opponent is on the verge of accepting, but has not finally agreed to, your position. You know that you must therefore increase your negotiating leverage. You can do this by disclosing the information about the new medical facility and skillfully relating how that facility will fit comfortably into your opponent's plans and desires to locate its new plant in an area that offers a unique environment for the company's management and employees. If your opponent was on the verge of finally agreeing to your position, it is highly likely this disclosure will be the final step necessary to make your pole long and strong enough to move your opponent favorably toward your negotiating objectives.

You might have accomplished the same result by other means such as injecting into the negotiation facts that are not favorable to your opponent, thus promoting fear on the opponent's part. If, for instance, you produced facts to show that there was another prospective purchaser seriously interested in the land, the opponent's resulting fear generated by the thought of losing one of the two choice sites may strongly motivate the opponent toward your negotiating objectives. And if the other prospective purchaser were a competitor of the opponent, the opponent's resulting fear of loss could be tremendous, thus increasing your leverage immensely.

As you read this book it is important to bear in mind this principle of leverage. By doing so you will discover not only numerous techniques that will increase leverage in addition to the two mentioned above but also you will be mindful of the fact that any skilled opponent will also be attempting to increase negotiating leverage and endeavor to motivate you toward the opponent's negotiating objectives. This awareness should better enable you to counter your opponent's attempts at increasing negotiating leverage, thereby enhancing your own chances of achieving negotiating success.

# CHAPTER 4

# Why an Accurate Conception of Power Is Essential to Consistent Negotiation Success

*Take time to think—it is a source of power.*

From an old Irish prayer

In every negotiation there are four conceptions of power that are vitally important for you to know. Two pertain directly to you, namely, your conception of the extent of your own negotiating power and your conception of the extent of your opponent's negotiating power. Two conceptions of power pertain directly to your opponent, namely, your opponent's conception of the extent of your negotiating power and your opponent's conception of the extent of his or her negotiating power.

Human minds, although physically similar, can differ widely in application. One person, for example, may react highly emotionally to a situation such as death whereas another person's reaction may be quite unemotional, even though both have the same relationship to the deceased. It is important for you, the negotiator, to always remain fully aware of these applicational differences so that you will carefully consider them in relationship to your opponent during your preparation for and during the actual negotiation. By doing so you will be more likely to arrive at an accurate judgment of the four conceptions of negotiating power at any given point in the negotiation, thus greatly enhancing your chances of attaining negotiation success.

## What Negotiators' Conception of Their Own Negotiating Power Should Be

During preparations for and in the course of any negotiation, regardless of the difficulty of the negotiation and the length and degree of preparation that is necessary, it is important for negotiators to carefully evaluate the strengths and weaknesses of their negotiating power. This is done by a careful and thorough examination and analysis of all matters relevant to the negotiation, including facts and law if a legal problem, and deciding if those matters are favorable to the negotiators' negotiating objectives (thus constituting potential negotiating power) or unfavorable (thus constituting potential lack of negotiating power). Only in that manner can negotiators *accurately* determine the extent of their power and how and when that power might be used in the negotiation. I emphasize the word "accurately" because it is a common error in negotiation for negotiators either to underestimate or overestimate the extent of their negotiating power. Either can work heavily to the negotiators' detriment.

For example, assume the negotiation involves two corporations. One manufactures a part that the other needs to complete assembly of a product the latter is going to market nationally. Bids for the part from numerous manufacturers have been taken by the purchasing corporation. The parts manufacturer has been in the business for a long period of time and has a very good idea of what its competition would charge for making the same part. Assume that the manufacturer knows that only one competitor can meet the manufacturer's price. Assume also that the purchasing corporation makes aggressive overtures toward entering into a contract with the manufacturer. These factors, namely, that the manufacturer can beat any competitive price except one and that the purchasing corporation is aggressively seeking an arrangement with the manufacturer, lead to the likely conclusion that the manufacturer has offered the lowest bid. Assuming that conclusion to be correct, the manufacturer can easily convert that knowledge into a source of negotiating power by tactfully conveying to the purchasing corporation the likelihood that the purchasing corporation may lose a contract with the manufacturer unless the purchasing corporation agrees with the manufacturer's proposals, perhaps proposals relating to delivery, payment terms, and numerous other facets involved in most business transactions. The fear created by the potential loss of its best source should motivate the purchasing corporation favorably toward the manufacturer's negotiating objectives.

Failure, on the other hand, of the manufacturing corporation to fully comprehend and appreciate its potential position of power would obviously work to the manufacturer's detriment. In such a situation, the manufacturer clearly lacks an accurate conception of its negotiating power based upon the developing facts. The net result is that it is "selling itself short" in the negotiations and thus making its negotiating road much more difficult to travel.

The moral is that in every negotiation it is vitally important for negotiators to take great care to fully analyze the elements of their own negotiating power. This analysis must take in both the periods prior to and during the actual negotiations. Negotiations are in a constant state of evolution with momentum often shifting between the negotiating parties like shifting sands of a desert. Negotiating power can dissipate just as quickly as it can develop and it is therefore important for negotiators to be constantly alert as the situation changes. Only by doing so can they possess a greater certainty that they are negotiating with full awareness of the true extent of their negotiating power. Moreover, negotiators will be better able to develop strategies and utilize techniques that take the greatest advantage of their negotiating power throughout the entire negotiation.

Negotiators must also bear in mind that a skillful opponent will fully analyze the negotiation and arrive at what the opponent feels are the negotiators' strongest elements of power. Failure of the negotiators to use any of those elements known to the opponent will immediately alert the opponent to the possibility that the negotiators lack either negotiating skill or preparation. The net result could be catastrophic to the negotiators. In such an event the opponent will develop greater boldness, in many cases increasing demands and even treating the negotiators with disdain. Without a doubt when that occurs, the chances of the negotiators accomplishing their negotiating objectives are, at best, very slim.

## What Negotiators' Conception of Their Opponent's Negotiating Power Should Be

In virtually every negotiation, negotiators are always exposed to forming their own conception of their opponent's negotiating power. In fact, forming their conception of their opponent's power is precisely what negotiators must do! Forming this conception enables negotiators to more effectively counter their opponent's power moves by adopting strategies and using techniques to suit the situation.

In forming this conception of the opponent's power, negotiators run a very real risk either of underestimating or overestimating the opponent's power, both prior to the negotiation when negotiators are considering strategies and techniques and also during the actual negotiation when negotiators must often form a conception of their opponent's negotiating power right on the spot.

There is no certain formula that will enable negotiators to reduce the chances that they will underestimate or overestimate the opponent's negotiating power. The greater experience the negotiators assemble, the more likely will be their chances of avoiding underestimation or overestimation. Even experienced negotiators, however, occasionally err. As a consequence, the only helpful recourse is to adopt a workable "rule of thumb" that operates to minimize errors, when and if they occur.

The rule of thumb that has proven most effective when negotiators are not certain of the extent of their opponent's negotiating power *is to overestimate their opponent's negotiating power rather than to underestimate it.* The reason is obvious. Underestimating an opponent's negotiating power, and adopting strategies and using techniques that are based upon the underestimation can result in considerable harm to the negotiators' position.

Contrast that to a situation in which an opponent's power has been overestimated. In this case the negotiators can be "pleasantly" surprised by discovering that their opponent's power is less than the negotiators supposed it to be.

To illustrate, assume the existence of a common occurrence, a dispute between a buyer and a seller over the sale of a product that the buyer claims is defective. Assume the seller is substantially wealthy. The buyer, however, is negotiating on the erroneous assumption that the opponent lacks wealth. That is, the buyer underestimates the opponent. Consequently, the buyer makes unreasonable demands, feeling that the opponent cannot incur the cost of going to court in the event of no settlement. The net result may be to substantially increase the likelihood of no favorable settlement of the dispute. If no settlement occurs, the shock could be considerable to the buyer who has underestimated the opponent and suddenly is in court facing a well-financed opponent.

Negotiating, on the other hand, on the basis that the seller possesses ample wealth to finance any litigation in the event of no suitable settlement will temper the buyer's demands and thus be more apt to facilitate a favorable agreement. If it turns out that the seller does possess ample wealth, no harm is done to the buyer's position since the buyer anticipated that. If the buyer later discovers that the seller, in fact, lacks sufficient wealth to pay for any litigation, no substantial damage has been done to the buyer. The buyer can easily adjust to the seller's lack of power and thus take full advantage of it.

The foregoing example illustrates the need in negotiations, particularly important ones, for the negotiator to be constantly on the alert for additional helpful information that will increase negotiating power. Discovery of facts that indicate a decrease of the opponent's negotiating power automatically results in an increase in the negotiator's negotiating power. It is very much like a teeter-totter with the opponent on the low end and the negotiator up in the air. Every bit of weight (power) lost by the opponent increases the negotiator's weight (power) thereby causing a reversal of the parties' positions.

## Why Negotiators Must Be Certain That Their Opponent Has a True Conception of the Negotiators' Power

Even the strongest army in the world could not fully motivate a weaker opponent to a favorable settlement without bloodshed if the weaker opponent was not completely aware of the strongest army's superior strength. Indeed, nations often like to parade their military might on special occasions in order to show other nations the extent of their strength and thus seek to favorably motivate those other nations. Similarly, any opponent who is not fully aware of the negotiators' negotiating power cannot be expected to be motivated favorably toward the negotiators' negotiating objectives.

Once negotiators fully comprehend the true extent of their own negotiating power, both prior to and during the actual negotiation, they must then be certain to take the second step of ensuring that their opponent fully comprehends the true extent of that power. If negotiators approach any negotiation, whether large or small, with this two-step process in mind, they will have a greater degree of assurance that they are using their negotiating power effectively.

Two people seldom see anything in the same way. Even two persons witnessing the same accident, for instance, will differ markedly when recounting it, and the more time that passes between the accident and the time they are asked to recall it, the greater the likelihood that their versions will differ. Recognizing this fact, negotiators must often take great pains to be certain that their opponent accurately knows the extent of the negotiators' negotiating power. If the opponent conceives that the negotiators possess an even greater degree of power than the negotiators actually do, this, of course, is an added bonus for the negotiators. But this luxury is not something that should be expected, particularly if the opponent is an experienced negotiator. The negotiators' objective is, therefore, to be certain that their opponent fully comprehends, at a minimum, the true extent of the negotiators' power on a consistent basis throughout the entire negotiation.

One of the best methods of accomplishing this objective is by use of repetition. Television commercials, since most are severly limited because of the expense of television time, employ repetition as a tool to get the viewer to remember the product, especially the product's name. Frequently, there are two or more persons in the commercial and they bandy the product's name about, or a new party may arrive and ask about the product. This inquiry invites the other players to repeat the product's name over and over throughout the duration of the commercial. In a recent commercial a product's name was mentioned 15 times in only one minute. Yet, it was done in such a skillful manner that the viewer was virtually unaware of the repetition. I was aware of the repetition only because I was consciously looking for it.

Constant repetition of the negotiators' power elements can be risky, especially if the opponent is an experienced negotiator. There is an adage that: "Knocking, in an individual, is just as much evidence of lack of power as it is in an automobile." Negotiators must therefore be particularly careful that their use of repetition does not work to their detriment and actually make the opponent misconstrue the repetition to indicate a lack of power.

## How the Opponent's Conception of His or Her Own Negotiating Power May Materially Affect the Final Negotiating Outcome

It is not uncommon, particularly when one negotiates on a regular basis, to encounter an opponent whose actions are temporarily unexplainable and even, on occasion, quite puzzling. The opponent may shout when it is inappropriate to shout, or pound the table and even threaten the negotiator with some sort of physical or economic harm if the negotiator doesn't go along with the opponent's position. Frequently, these actions are the result of bluffing, inexperience, poor negotiating habits, and even haste. If the actions are the result of any of these, they are easy to detect and deal with. Often, however, they are the outward manifestations of an opponent who feels that he or she has ample power to dictate the terms of the negotiations. These circumstances often occur, for example, in supply–demand situations in which the demand for or supply of a product or services such as professional services disproportionately exceeds the supply or demand and the buyer or seller is told, in essence, to "take it or leave it." On numerous such occasions, the opponent may not in fact possess such power even though the opponent thinks he or she does.

Whatever the case, the opponent's confidence fostered by the *belief* that he or she possesses such great negotiating power may have a material affect on the final negotiating outcome. The outcome of the negotiation may be a victory for the opponent won through "browbeating" the negotiator into submission. Or the negotiation may end in a failure to reach any type of agreement because the negotiator reacted negatively to the opponent's strong-arm tactics.

Conversely, an opponent who believes he or she lacks negotiating power may outwardly show pessimism. Maybe the opponent does really possess strong negotiating power but is unaware of it. The opponent may be unaware of his or her true negotiating power for a variety of reasons such as lack of experience, failure to adequately research the facts, or the laws, or even failure to spend the necessary time to think out the matter. Whatever the case, the opponent's negotiating attitude will substantially hamper him or her and will thus play an important role in the final negotiating outcome.

It is important for the negotiator to be constantly on the alert in trying to determine the opponent's conception of the opponent's own negotiating power. If the negotiator discovers that the opponent conceives his or her own negotiating power as being great when in fact the negotiator knows it is otherwise, it is a simple matter for the negotiator to adopt strategies and use techniques that are designed to apprise the opponent of the true extent of the opponent's power, thereby materially reducing the opponent's effectiveness in most negotiating situations. It is almost always very deflating for most people to discover that they posses less of a good thing than they originally thought. Making this "discovery" in the heat of negotiation often has even a greater negative impact on the individual making the discovery.

To illustrate, assume the negotiation involves an employment contract and the potential employee is holding out for what the potential employer feels is an exorbitantly high salary. The potential employee's confidence is boosted primarily by the knowledge that he or she has been doing an outstanding job for his or her present employer and is therefore very bold in making demands. "I've got the track record," the employee thinks. "Why not capitalize on it?"

Assume the potential employer initially believes the potential employee's track record to be as good as the potential employee conceives it to be but later, through tactful inquiry from other sources, learns that it is not that great but that the employee is still good enough to do the job. Tactfully attacking the potential employee's past performance so as to not completely deflate the employee but merely to reduce the employee's demands can be easily done with this newly acquired knowledge.

**The Best Time for the Negotiator to Determine the Opponent's Conception of the Opponent's Negotiating Power**

During preparation for the negotiation is the best time to learn as much as possible about an opponent's conception of the opponent's own negotiating power. This can be done in a variety of ways. You might draw on past experiences with the same opponent if you have previously negotiated with the opponent or with others within the same organization who are likely to negotiate in a similar fashion; you might tactfully inquire from others who may have had a negotiating experience with the opponent or even ferret out information from other sources such as the library or any organization the opponent may belong to; or you might simply make assumptions based upon the opponent's age, years of experience, educational background, and other similar facets. The point is that the more you learn about your opponent, the more likely you will be able to accurately gauge your opponent's way of thinking and thus judge your opponent's conception of his or her own negotiating power.

Combining this previously acquired knowledge with precise observation during the actual negotiation often brings surprising results when you attempt to read the opponent's conception of his or her own power.

If your opponent overestimates the extent of his or her negotiating power, it may be a simple task for you to play along until the opponent has climbed completely out on a limb by committing himself or herself to a position whose foundation is based upon the opponent's faulty conception of the extent of his or her negotiating power. Then you produce a saw in the form of facts to indicate that the opponent, in reality, lacks such power, and eagerly eye the limb on which the opponent is perched.

For example, I was involved in a complex negotiation involving many issues. One issue was the value of a large parcel of real estate with a building on it. The property had to be evaluated for tax purposes. The property had been sold just prior to the negotiating session. My opponent was unaware of the sale and immediately launched into a detailed analysis of why the price he sought was correct. He didn't really give me an opportunity to inform him of the sale price which was for a much lower figure than what he was quoting. It was clear that he had done considerable work on the matter and was highly confident of his position. As he talked on he was eventually able to discern from my expressions and interest in what he was saying that he was out on a limb. Finally he asked: "Has there been a sale?"

"Yes," I replied. "The sale price is much lower."

We agreed that the sale price represented the correct value. More importantly, my opponent became very timid on subsequent issues as a result of his overestimation of power on the property value issue. The net result was considerable loss of negotiating power for him on virtually every remaining issue involved in the negotiation.

**The Necessity for Probing an Opponent's Silence**

During a heated discussion at a board of directors meeting one member of the board sat quietly amid the furious argument and table-pounding.

Later, he was told by the board chairperson, "I want to compliment you. You kept your cool in there when all the others were blowing their tops. How did you do it?"

"Well," confessed the serene member, "I simply did not understand what anyone else was talking about."

In negotiation, it is not uncommon for an opponent to fail to fully comprehend what you are advocating. When that occurs, your negotiating power is being dissipated. The opponent's silence is often the tip-off that he or she doesn't understand. Accordingly, if an opponent remains unusually silent when you feel the opponent should be talking, you would be wise to probe into the reason for the silence. This probing can be done directly simply by asking the opponent whether there are any questions, or indirectly, by slipping in thoughts or comments related to the negotiation that you have strong reason to believe will call for a reply from the opponent. If no reply is forthcoming, lack of understanding may be the cause of the opponent's silence and you should undertake remedial steps by making an effort to simpify your presentation or suggesting a postponement in order to allow yourself sufficient time to work out a more simplified presentation. Failure to undertake such remedial action could lead to a substantial loss of your negotiating power as a result of the opponent's failure to understand your position.

# CHAPTER 5

# Facts Are the Foundation on Which to Build Solid Negotiating Power

*Get the facts, or the facts will get you. And when you get 'em, get 'em right, or they will get you wrong.*

Fuller

A very common error and great source of loss of negotiating power can be your failure to get complete and accurate facts relative to the subject matter of the negotiation. To negotiate without complete and accurate facts is to be very much like the foolish man in the Bible* who built his house on sand only to have it fall when exposed to water and wind. Just as the house fell, your negotiating power will dissipate once your opponent discovers that you lack complete and accurate facts. The reason is quite simple. Positions you advocate or advance that are based upon incomplete or inaccurate facts are bound to be faulty positions that can, once their faults are exposed, quickly switch the negotiating momentum to the opponent and make it very difficult for you to regain the momentum you enjoyed prior to exposure.

To illustrate the importance of getting complete and accurate facts, many years ago when I was beginning my negotiating career I was involved in negotiating the value of many different kinds and sizes of businesses. One business was a gasoline service station. I analyzed fully the station's profit-and-loss statement and balance sheet and even had an appraisal of the physical structure and land. But I lacked one essential fact. It seemed that the business was located in

---

*Matthew* 7:26 and 27

an area that was quickly deteriorating. I learned that several gasoline stations in that area had gone out of business recently. As a consequence, in spite of the favorable financial statements and the appraisal, it was clear that future prospects for the business were not too bright and that the future value of the business must be determined by a consideration of all of the factors including the rapid deterioration of the area in which the business was situated. From that point on, in order to have a complete and accurate factual picture, I made it a set policy to visit the site of any business I had to evaluate financially.

This policy paid dividends rather quickly. Soon thereafter I was involved in the valuation of a business that was earning substantial profits through manufacturing a much sought-after product. As a consequence, the business should normally have had a very high value. This time I visited the plant only to find that both the plant building and equipment were in such a deteriorated and sorry condition that soon a substantial investment of millions of dollars would be necessary in order to remedy the situation. It seemed that the business owners had neglected replenishing the business property in order to maximize profits. Future profits, of course, would be substantially depressed in order to pay for or service the debt necessary to bring the plant and equipment back up to a new or dependable condition.

In still another case, the negotiation issue concerned the value of an apartment building. A careful reading of the building appraisal left me with the impression that the structure was relatively small and insignificant. When I visited the property and first laid eyes on it, however, I couldn't believe I was looking at the same property that was dealt with in the appraisal and I actually rechecked the address to be certain I was looking at the same property. It was very large and in very good condition and obviously worth considerably more than the appraisal would have led one to believe. Armed with this significant fact, I found it a relatively simple matter to get a valuation increase from my opponent.

**Always Be Certain to Distinguish between Facts and Hearsay**

Hearsay is information not acquired from personal knowledge but rather from what has been heard from others. It is therefore second-hand information. Obviously, negotiators are exposed to large doses of hearsay, almost all of which is claimed to be factually accurate. Some of it may be accurate and very useful in the negotiation. Much of it, however, will be inaccurate or incomplete and therefore potentially highly detrimental if relied upon and used by the negotiator. It thus becomes very important for the negotiator, in a quest for facts, to be certain to distinguish between what is accurate and what is inaccurate hearsay.

The real necessity for this microscopic analysis is to be certain that only reliable hearsay is actually used in the negotiation. There is no quicker way for you to severely damage your credibility and thus dissipate your negotiating power than to discover, perhaps from your opponent, that the hearsay you used is inaccurate.

It is important to always bear in mind that the opponent may be relying upon inaccurate hearsay. When you know or have strong reason to suspect this to be the case, you should check it out. If your investigation confirms that the opponent is using inaccurate information, you are afforded an excellent opportunity to strategically point this out to your opponent and thus quickly increase your negotiating power by placing your opponent on the defensive. Remember, once the opponent is on the defensive, it is virtually impossible for him or her to gain any bargaining edge. Negotiating power cannot be based upon or sustained by use of inaccurate information. Frequently, you will discover that the opponent is not even aware of the information's inaccuracy because of not having taken the time and effort to verify its correctness. Accordingly, it is always wise for you to pay particularly close attention to any factual information used by your opponent, especially when the negotiation is an important one or the factual information relied upon by the opponent is a very important, perhaps a critical, element to the outcome of the negotiation.

## CHAPTER 6

# Power Techniques— The Instruments of Negotiating Power

*Knowledge is only potential power. It becomes power only when, and if, it is organized into definite plans of action and directed to a definite end.*

Napoleon Hill

In 1899, when James B. Duke was building his American Tobacco trust, he summoned R. J. Reynolds, a competitor, to his hotel room and said: "I'll give you one million for two-thirds of your company or I'll break you. Take your choice." Reynolds replied: "My price is three million. Otherwise, for every dollar you cost me, I'm going to cost American Tobacco a hundred." Reynolds got the three million.

There is often great confusion as to precisely what constitutes a negotiating technique and when a technique should be used in any negotiation. Resolving this confusion is obviously of primary importance. Otherwise, you cannot expect to skillfully employ negotiating techniques on a consistently successful basis.

**Negotiation Techniques—What They Are and How to Use Them**

Stated simply, a negotiation technique is a method or means of carrying out a plan of operation. Techniques should be designed to *motivate your opponent favorably toward your negotiating objectives.* Techniques are therefore the real instruments of negotiating power.

If we make some assumptions, the encounter between Duke and Reynolds can be used to further illustrate and illuminate what negotiating techniques are and how to use them. Let's assume that

Reynolds, prior to meeting with Duke, knew that the chances were good that Duke would offer either to buy Reynolds out or to drive him out of business. Duke had apparently done the same thing to other companies. As a consequence, Reynolds had to decide whether to sell out to Duke or to resist any efforts by Duke to drive him out of business. Assume that Reynolds concluded that he did not desire to fight Duke on a long-term basis since Duke would probably succeed in driving him out of business if he refused to sell. Reynolds therefore adopted as his negotiation objective a sale of his company *at his price.*

Reynolds had to next come up with a negotiation strategy that would enable him to accomplish his objective. Assume he knew that Duke would spare no expense in driving a competitor out of business, but that he also knew that Duke was a very wise and prudent businessman who was not likely to entangle himself in a corporate battle that could be too costly in relation to the asking price for the company. In addition, Reynolds felt that Duke very likely knew that Reynolds was a determined person who "says what he means and means what he says." Reynolds therefore decided to adopt a negotiation strategy that was consistent with these assumptions.

**The "Greater Fear" Power Negotiating Technique**

Taken literally, fear is an emotion that normally causes people to react sometimes favorably and at other times unfavorably to their own best interests. When Duke gave Reynolds the ultimatum of selling a two-thirds interest for one million dollars or be broken, Duke was attempting to create fear in Reynolds in order for Duke to accomplish his objective.

Attempting to play upon an opponent's fear is a common strategy in negotiation. To illustrate by using what is virtually an everyday occurrence, assume that a man goes into an automobile showroom to look at new cars that are advertised at a considerable discount. He finds a car he likes but needs time to think about it. The sales agent advises that the discount prices will be discontinued in two days and that the man had better get in his order or he will lose out. What the sales agent is trying to do is to create fear of loss in the man. The sales agent is thus employing fear as a negotiating strategy to speed up the sale.

Playing on a negotiator's fear seldom works against skilled negotiators because they ordinarily anticipate the weaknesses in their negotiating positions and the potential strategies and techniques to be used by their opponents, and take steps to remedy them. That is precisely what Reynolds did. Knowing that Duke would probably attempt to intimidate him into selling at Duke's price, Reynolds similarly decided to employ a strategy of using fear. But Reynolds' strategy was much more effective because his opponent, Duke, did not anticipate that Duke's use of fear would be actually converted to negotiating power by his opponent, Reynolds.

In order to accomplish this conversion, Reynolds turned to the power negotiating technique of impressing a greater fear into Duke by informing Duke that it would cost his company one hundred dollars for every dollar it cost Reynolds. The net result was to motivate Duke toward Reynolds' negotiating objective of receiving three million instead of one million dollars.

Note the difference between a negotiating strategy and a technique. Duke's negotiating objective was to buy a two-thirds interest in Reynolds' company for one million. Duke decided to motivate Reynolds toward Duke's negotiating objective by employing a strategy that would make Reynolds fearful of having his company literally run out of business.

Reynolds' objective was to get three million dollars. He, too, decided to employ a strategy of fear. He then reverted to the power negotiating technique of impressing a "Greater Fear," waiting until Duke led out with his threat or ultimatum and then hitting Duke with declarations that would cause Duke to experience even greater fear of being forced to engage in a corporate battle that would be more costly than paying Reynolds the three million dollars.

## When the "Greater Fear" Power Negotiating Technique Should Be Used

There are certain conditions that should exist prior to using the "Greater Fear" power negotiating technique. The most obvious among them is that use of this technique should come only after your opponent has attempted to impress a fear in you. It is therefore a trailing technique. Nevertheless, the fact that it comes after the opponent's initial use of fear does not detract from its effectiveness as evidenced by the dramatic results achieved by Reynolds.

Second, the technique works best when your opponent knows or has strong reason to believe that you possess the capability to carry out whatever you claim you can do. In order to give in, Duke obviously must either have known or had strong reason to believe that Reynolds was fully capable of carrying out his threat that for every dollar it cost Reynolds it would cost Duke a hundred dollars. If Duke had no such knowledge or had strong reason to believe that Reynolds was not capable of carrying out his threat, Reynolds would have found it virtually impossible to successfully employ the technique. It therefore follows that whenever you use this technique, you must have strong reason to believe that your opponent has knowledge of the fact that you are fully capable of carrying out whatever you say you will do that causes your opponent to have greater fear. If you feel that your opponent is not likely to possess knowledge of your capabilities, it is important for you to take whatever steps necessary to be certain that your opponent has such knowledge before you use the technique.

**When You Use the "Greater Fear" Technique, Don't Bluff**

Bluffing is as common in negotiation as it is in poker. But if you desire to become skilled at negotiating, you should not rely upon bluffing as the road to success. If when relating the facts or circumstances that create a "Greater Fear" in your opponent, you are bluffing and are not really capable of carrying it out, your opponent has only to tactfully call a temporary halt to the negotiation in order to find out whether you do, in fact, possess such capability. If the opponent's detective work leads him or her to the conclusion that you are bluffing, not only will the opponent not experience a greater fear but the opponent will probably experience no fear at all. It is also highly unlikely that the opponent will take you seriously throughout the rest of the negotiation. The net result of such a situation could be a complete loss of your credibility and thus a material impairment of your negotiating power.

# CHAPTER 7

# The "Rainy Day" Power Negotiating Technique

*How much pain the evils have cost us that have never happened!*
Thomas Jefferson

There is a story that travels throughout the legal profession about a jury of 12 men, 11 of whom were active farmers and the twelfth, a retired farmer. These 12 jurors listened attentively to the case before them and then retired to deliberate a verdict. The 11 working farmers were for a verdict of guilty. The retired farmer was for a verdict of not guilty. It was necessary that the verdict be unanimous. The 11 jurors worked diligently throughout most of the day trying to convince their retired colleague to switch to a guilty verdict so they could all get home to take in thier hay before the rain began that had been forecasted for later that afternoon. The retired juror, however, resisted all efforts and just sat looking out of the window at the dark rain clouds as they slowly approached. As precious time dragged on the 11 active farmers showed increasing signs of nervousness and finally, at the first clap of thunder, panicked and all changed their votes to not guilty.

## Why the "Rainy Day" Technique Is So Effective

It is a statistical fact that most negotiations, particularly those that are highly controversial, are settled at or near a set deadline. Yet it is not uncommon to find numerous negotiators that fail to set deadlines.

When a deadline is initially set, ordinarily there is very little anxiety experienced by the negotiator's opponent unless the deadline is almost immediate. The reason is that the amount of anxiety ordinarily experienced by anyone is normally inversely proportionate to the remoteness of the thing that is feared.

For example, an individual may not fear death because the possibility of dying may be too remote. But if the same individual were advised by a doctor about having a terminal illness that would kill within a month, the anxiety the individual would experience could be tremendous.

So, if the deadline set by the negotiator is imminent, the opponent may experience immediate anxiety. If, on the other hand, the deadline is a long way off, the initial anxiety experienced by the opponent may not be that great. As the deadline approaches, however, the opponent's anxiety may continue to build and reach its peak just before the deadline arrives. That is precisely why so many negotiations are settled at or near a set deadline and why the "rainy day" technique is such a powerful motivator that should be included in every negotiator's arsenal of power negotiating techniques.

To illustrate, during the 12-day Camp David summit negotiations between Egypt's President Anwar Sadat, Israel's Prime Minister Menachem Begin, and President Jimmy Carter, little progress was made toward arriving at a settlement of the difficult issues that had divided Egypt and Israel for 30 years. Finally, a Sunday deadline was imposed and the parties, as the deadline approached, began to make considerable progress toward settlement of some of the issues. As the deadline grew closer, the parties made more and more progress until substantial ground was covered toward a final settlement.

This occurrence between the great nations of Egypt, Israel, and the United States is a very good illustration of the fact that the "rainy day" technique, together with all of the other strategies and techniques set forth in this book, can be applied to virtually any negotiation, including those of the greatest importance such as the Camp David summit negotiations. The common denominator of people ensures such a universal application.

**Common Pitfalls to Avoid When Using the "Rainy Day" Technique**

There is a story about a tough, old cowhand who sauntered into a saloon and began drinking whiskey by the bottle. The more he drank the more unruly he became, shooting holes in the ceiling and floor and letting loose with a barrage of insults at anyone and everyone in the saloon. Everybody was afraid to take on the old cowhand. Finally, the town's little, mild-mannered storekeeper walked up to the unruly cowhand and said, "I'll give you five minutes to get out of town." The old cowhand holstered his gun, pushed the whiskey bottle away, briskly walked out, got on his horse, and rode out of town. When he left, someone asked the little storekeeper what he would have done if the unruly cowhand had refused to go. "I'd have extended the deadline," he said.

The moral, of course, is that in order for the "rainy day" technique to be effective, the negotiator must be fully prepared to live with the consequences of any time limit set. Extending a set time limit should be done *only* when there are *significant* new matters that justify an extension. Otherwise, the negotiator's arbitrary time extensions will completely insulate the opponent from any anxiety, not only when deadlines are set but also as the time for each deadline approaches. In addition, the negotiator may be in danger of developing the reputation of being a "deadline extender" and thus deprive himself or herself from ever effectively using the "rainy day" technique.

## Deadlines Inadvertently Set by an Opponent

Frequently your opponent will subject himself or herself to the "rainy day" technique without realizing it. This is where your concentration and alertness really pay off. Often, for instance, the opponent may say, "I must catch a plane in an hour" or "I have an important conference in an hour." Declarations such as these are, in essence, self-imposed deadlines and increase your negotiating power. It is a simple matter for you, for instance, to wait until the self-imposed deadline is near and the opponent is experiencing the greatest anxiety to get away, and then say something such as: "I think my proposal is very fair. Why don't we settle this and you can be on your way with a free mind." It is not uncommon for the opponent to say, sometimes in sheer desperation to get away, "OK."

Just as opponents frequently set self-imposed deadlines, so might negotiators make the same error. Hence, it is important for the good negotiator to remain fully aware of this possibility and to take great care to avoid it.

### Deadlines Set by Circumstances or "Acts of God"

The story about the 12 juror farmers is a good example of deadlines set by circumstances and an Act of God. The circumstance was that 11 of them had to take in their hay. The rain, of course, was the Act of God.

Circumstances that act as deadline setters abound in life. Late or cancelled airplane flights, transportation strikes, and illness are some examples of deadlines imposed by circumstances. Contract expiration dates are other good examples. True, in the late or cancelled flight situation, the strike, illness, and even the contract expiration date, the opponent can work to set a new time. But often this is not done and even when it is, it operates in many instances to make a settlement even more imperative since the parties are working "on borrowed time."

### Deadlines Set by Your Opponent

Obviously, opponents set deadlines too and it is therefore incumbent on you to alleviate to the greatest extent possible any anxiety caused by the opponent's deadline setting. If the deadline set by the opponent is an arbitrary one, it is usually fairly easy for you to request more time *at the time the deadline is set.* In most instances, the opponent will oblige and set the deadline for the time you request. If the opponent refuses to extend the deadline or has set what the opponent believes is a realistic, and not an arbitrary, deadline, you must be fully prepared to meet the deadline. In these situations, you should not procrastinate and allow yourself to fall victim to the "rainy day" technique. Rather, you should use the time up to the deadline to calmly analyze and decide whether you want to exercise whatever rights or options you have as a result of the deadline.

For example, assume the opponent represents the owner of real estate that you desire to purchase. Your opponent gives you ten days in which to make a decision to purchase the land at the price offered by the opponent. You should undertake careful analysis prior to the expiration of the ten-day period and, if you think the price may be too high and want to make an offer at a lower price, you should normally convey the counteroffer to the opponent as soon as possible, well before the ten-day deadline date. This, in essence, operates to eliminate the deadline (unless your counteroffer is rejected by the opponent and the original ten-day deadline is restated) and also any hazard of falling victim to the "rainy day" technique.

CHAPTER 8

# The "Exhausting" Power Negotiating Technique

*How poor are they that have no patience. What wound did ever heal but by degrees?*

Shakespeare

A number of years ago I encountered several experienced negotiators who had a very strong negotiating position. My position, by contrast, was very weak. It was obvious from the initial negotiating session that my opponents were fully aware of the strength of their position, knew it thoroughly, and were going to present it forcefully. They had no intention of allowing me to get a decent foothold in the discussions. It also became clear during our initial meeting, as a consequence of my opponents' strong approach, that more than one negotiating session must be held to achieve success. I decided to carry on the negotiation on a session-by-session basis hoping that my opponents would exhaust their negotiating power. The negotiation continued for six sessions. My opponents were particularly disturbed that they could not make an impression strong enough to attain their objectives and finally became more receptive to my presentation, losing sight of much of the strength of their case. If the pattern could have been diagrammed, it would look something like Fig. 8.1.

Note that by the sixth session the point of exhaustion had been virtually reached. I had gained considerable power simply because my opponents had lost theirs. The bulk of my power was derived from using the "exhausting" technique. After the sixth negotiating session, I could truly begin to present my case, knowing that my opponents would be in their most receptive state of mind.

40    Chapter 8

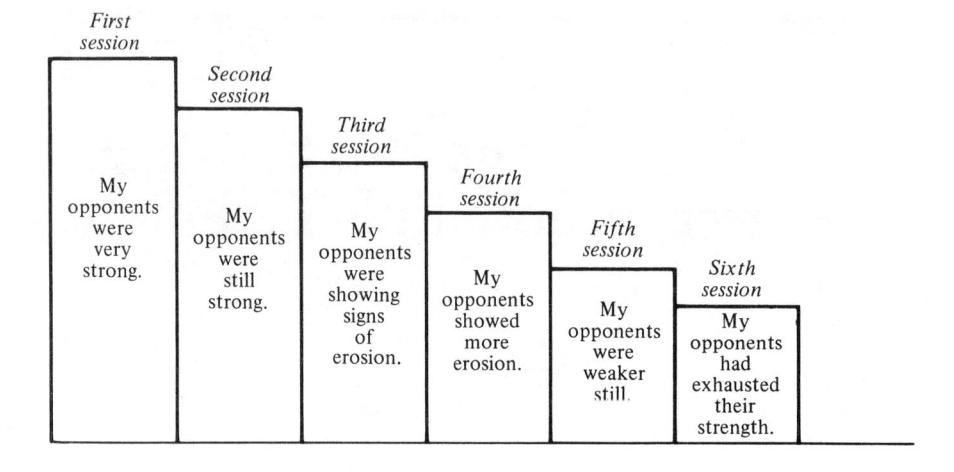

```
┌─────────┐
│  First  │
│ session │
│         │┌─────────┐
│   My    ││ Second  │
│opponents││ session │
│  were   │├─────────┤┌─────────┐
│  very   ││   My    ││  Third  │
│ strong. ││opponents││ session │
│         ││  were   │├─────────┤┌─────────┐
│         ││  still  ││   My    ││ Fourth  │
│         ││ strong. ││opponents││ session │
│         ││         ││  were   │├─────────┤┌─────────┐
│         ││         ││ showing ││   My    ││  Fifth  │
│         ││         ││  signs  ││opponents││ session │
│         ││         ││   of    ││ showed  │├─────────┤┌─────────┐
│         ││         ││ erosion.││  more   ││   My    ││  Sixth  │
│         ││         ││         ││ erosion.││opponents││ session │
│         ││         ││         ││         ││  were   │├─────────┤
│         ││         ││         ││         ││ weaker  ││   My    │
│         ││         ││         ││         ││  still. ││opponents│
│         ││         ││         ││         ││         ││  had    │
│         ││         ││         ││         ││         ││exhausted│
│         ││         ││         ││         ││         ││ their   │
│         ││         ││         ││         ││         ││strength.│
└─────────┴┴─────────┴┴─────────┴┴─────────┴┴─────────┴┴─────────┘
```

Figure 8.1

**Dealing with Overly Aggressive Opponents**

Frequently in negotiation the negotiator will encounter an opponent who is overly aggressive. The opponent may exhibit this aggression in a variety of ways—talking in a loud voice, standing instead of sitting, or glaring at the negotiator in a confident, even defiant manner. Attempting to motivate such a confident opponent favorably toward the negotiator's negotiating objectives is a very difficult task. An aggressive opponent wants and intends to get his or her way and is not inclined to agree to the ways of others.

The "exhausting" technique is an excellent method to defeat aggressive opponents. As the negotiation draws on, the opponent's confidence and aggressiveness subside to a great extent and the opponent becomes much more receptive to the negotiator's positions. The net result is an increase in the negotiator's negotiating power.

**When the "Exhausting" Technique Works Best**

Whenever the negotiator consciously decides to extend the negotiation in order to allow the opponent to become exhausted, the negotiator becomes insulated against the opponent's presentation. The negotiator deliberately allows the opponent to proceed without paying any particular attention to the substance of what the opponent is saying.

There is always a danger that the opponent will simply break off the negotiations, largely out of frustration at being unable to convince the negotiator of the merits of the opponent's cause early in the negotiation. As the negotiations drag on, this danger becomes more acute in those negotiations in which it is not mandatory that the negotiating parties reach an agreement. As a consequence, even though the "exhausting" technique can work well in nonmandatory negotiations if practiced skillfully, its best use is in those negotiations in which the negotiating parties *must* reach an agreement. Prime examples of such mandatory negotiations are company–union or governmental–union negotiations.

Many negotiations are also mandatory because of the strong desire of the parties to acquire the subject matter of the negotiation. It is therefore always wise for the negotiator to carefully remain alert to determine how badly the opponent wants to conclude the negotiation favorably. If a very strong desire to do so is detected, the chances are very good that the "exhausting" technique will work very well if the negotiator concludes that the opponent has a strong negotiating position that needs exhausting.

For example, in many negotiations involving the sale of homes, cars, boats, businesses, and unique items such as antiques, the prospective purchaser or seller may have a strong desire to successfully acquire or sell the item. In all of these situations, therefore, there is a very good possibility of using the "exhausting" technique when the seller or the buyer, as the case may be, has the stronger negotiating position.

# CHAPTER 9

# The "Paper Stack" Power Negotiating Technique

*All power is a compound of time and patience.*

Old proverb

Eleven out of 12 directors of a large corporation sat around a polished, oval-shaped table. In front of each of them was nothing except a pad and pencil. The twelfth director, however, had several large stacks of papers in front of him. Each stack was almost a foot high. As a heated argument ensued between the directors over an important change in the corporation's policy, the 11 sparsely equipped directors glanced frequently at their colleague with the papers stacked in front of him, as if waiting for him to speak out. He remained, however, attentive but silent. Finally, after the matter had been thoroughly hashed and rehashed, the chairperson of the board asked the silent director for his opinion. He voiced his opinion, at the same time referring to a paper that he took from the top of one of the piles in front of him. A brief discussion was held and the board unanimously adopted the "silent" director's suggested approach.

After the meeting adjourned, the chairperson of the board approached the "silent" director and thanked him for his contribution and for coming to the meeting so thoroughly prepared. "Oh," replied the director, "most of those papers had nothing to do with the directors' meeting. They were merely old files my secretary dropped off for me to look at before we threw them away. I was going to take them with me on my vacation immediately after the board meeting

43

was over and look them over then. The only one that was relevant to the discussion was the paper that I took from the top that contained notes that I made during the course of the board's discussions."

"Things are seldom what they seem." This adage has even greater impact when the circumstances are out of the ordinary. In the directors' story, all of the directors were accustomed to meeting with only pads and pencils before them, not stacks of data. This is frequently the case because most corporate directors are normally from outside of the company and therefore not prepared to spend great amounts of time analyzing each matter to come before the board. Rather, the directors rely heavily upon corporate management and other experts to apprise them prior to the board meeting or by summarizing memos as to what is precisely involved. The director with the stacks of papers in front of him therefore represented a departure from this established practice and gave the impression, although unwarranted, that he was better prepared and possessed greater knowledge of the subject under discussion. It was, consequently, natural and logical for the other directors not only to seek his judgment but also rely upon it concerning the proper course to follow.

**Use of the "Paper Stack" Technique in Negotiation**

There is an essential difference between using the paper stack technique in negotiation and the directors' story. In negotiation, all of the stacked data that is visible for the opponent to see *must be relevant to the negotiation.* Bluffing by adding to the stack papers that are immaterial can be devastating to the credibility of the negotiator if the ploy is discovered. And make no mistake about it, once the negotiator's credibility has been damaged, any chances of prevailing in the negotiation are substantially decreased. In fact, it is strongly urged that you, the negotiator, do nothing that would even hint at running the risk of damaging your negotiating credibility. The data that makes up the stacks must therefore be relevant to the negotiation.

To illustrate, I was involved in a complex negotiation in which my files, if stacked in one pile, would have been over three feet high. I placed all of the files in three neat stacks to my immediate right and allowed them to stay there during the entire course of the negotiation. The large stacks were motivating my opponent toward my negotiating objectives by telegraphing the full impact of my preparation and knowledge of the subject matter of the negotiation. The stacks therefore became a source of negotiating power on which I was able to fully capitalize.

### The Best Time to Use the "Paper Stack" Technique

Compatibility is an important element in most negotiations. The more easily and naturally you can use power negotiating techniques, the greater are your chances of favorably motivating your opponent toward your negotiating objectives.

The best time to use the "paper stack" technique is at the outset of the negotiation when the parties are sitting down for the first time. The reason is that if the negotiation is well under way and you then proceed to stack data in front of you or you have the data stacked in front of you at subsequent negotiating sessions when the data was absent at the initial negotiating session, your opponent may become curious and suspicious, not so much as to what is in the stacked data but *why* the data is being stacked at this juncture of the negotiation. The stacked data loses much of its impact by forcing the opponent to concentrate on "why" the data has now been produced and the opponent's attention is diverted from what the data itself represents, namely, that your knowledge and preparation are great.

Once you have decided to use the "paper stack" technique, it is important that you continue to use the technique throughout the entire negotiation unless there is ample reason for abandoning its use and that reason is either apparent or has been fully explained to your opponent.

For example, assume you have used the technique throughout the first several sessions of the negotiation. Most of the important issues have been favorably resolved and only a few minor issues remain. You might now abandon the "paper stack" technique without risk of adverse effects by advising your opponent in a light sort of way: "Now that we've got the heavy issues out of the way, I don't have to carry all of this data around." Or, perhaps the site of the negotiations has been changed and you can explain the absence of the large stacks of data by saying that it is too much of an effort to carry "all of those heavy data with me." Whatever the case, you should never take it for granted that your opponent is fully aware of the reason for the absence of the paper stacks and should make tactful efforts to justify their absence in order to be certain that your opponent is fully aware of the genuine reason for their absence.

**Use of the "Paper Stack" Technique When
Negotiating on Your Opponent's Home Field**

Although you should strive to negotiate on your own home field or, if that is not possible, at some neutral location, often neither is possible and you must negotiate on your opponent's home field. When that occurs, you may face a logistics problem in transporting the paper stack data, particularly if you must employ public transportation to get to the negotiation site. Carting extensive data may prove burdensome and there may be risk of loss. In addition, carting the data may cause your opponent to suspect that you are merely trying to use the data to influence him or her. Accordingly, it is important for you to take along as part of your paper stack only data to which you are likely to refer during the negotiation. Actual use of the data will reduce your opponent's suspicion that the data is for "show" only and not really relevant and necessary to the negotiation. It also reinforces your credibility which, as stated earlier, is essential to attaining consistent negotiation success.

CHAPTER 10

# The "War and Peace" Power Negotiating Technique

*The mind of man is fond of power; increase his prospects and you enlarge his desires.*

Gouverneur Morris

Howard Hughes, the legendary billionaire, wanted to negotiate a large contract to purchase airplanes. There were 34 items that Hughes wanted to have in the contract. Eleven of the 34 items were "musts." Hughes began the negotiations personally with a representative of the airplane manufacturer. Discussions got so heated that Hughes was literally "kicked off" the premises. Hughes then sent his personal representative to continue the negotiations. Hughes told his representative that if he could get the 11 "musts" in the contract, Hughes would be satisfied. Hughes's representative got 30 out of the 34 items, including all of the 11 "musts." When asked how he did it, the representative replied: "Simple. Every time we came to a sticky point, I said, . . . 'Do you want to settle this thing with me, or do you want another dose of Howard Hughes.' And every time he said, 'All right, you can have it!' "*

**Important Requirements of Using the "War and Peace" Power Negotiating Technique**

From the Hughes example, we learn that in order to use the "war and peace" technique, there must be two negotiators. The first

---

*\*Howard, The Amazing Mr. Hughes,* by Noah Dietrich with Bob Thomas. Fawcett, 1972, pp. 223–224.

47

negotiator begins the negotiation alone. If both negotiators were present at the outset the hostility created during the initial negotiating session by the first negotiator may spill over onto the second negotiator, thus making it highly improbable that the second negotiator will be able to return to the negotiation alone at a later session and obtain any realistic results.

At the initial negotiating session, the first negotiator literally makes "war" on the opponent, falling short, however, of actually forcing the opponent to break off the negotiation. The net effect of the first negotiator's antics is to soften the opponent to such an extent that it is painful for the opponent to even visualize continuing the negotiations with the first negotiator.

At this point, the second negotiator enters the negotiation, quietly and tactfully conducting the negotiation in a peaceful manner but always with the threat of having the first negotiator reenter the negotiation should the opponent not come to terms with the second negotiator. If this technique is handled skillfully, its net result is often as dramatic as it was in the Howard Hughes experience.

### The Type of Negotiations in Which the "War and Peace" Technique Works Best

Because the "war" made by the first negotiator forces the opponent to recoil mentally from the substance of the discussions while in the presence of the first negotiator, it follows that the "war and peace" technique should be used primarily in those negotiations in which the opponent is strongly interested in concluding an arrangement with the negotiator and therefore is unlikely to completely break off the negotiation when set upon by the first negotiator. It is therefore important for the negotiator to weigh carefully how much importance the opponent attaches to concluding an arrangement with the negotiator. Chances of a complete breakoff of the negotiation are very real if the opponent is not greatly interested in concluding an arrangement with the negotiator and is set upon by the first negotiator at the initial negotiating session.

### The Best Place to Use the "War and Peace" Technique

Contrary to the general rule that the ideal place to conduct the negotiation is on the negotiator's home field or, if that is not possible, at a neutral place, use of the "war and peace" power negotiating technique works best on the opponents' home field. The reason is that the psychological security afforded the opponents by being on their home field tends to offset the "war" being waged upon them by the first negotiator. The first negotiator is the one who is either forced off or voluntarily departs the opponents' premises, leaving the opponents disposed to receive the second negotiator. Contrast that to a situation in which the opponents are negotiating on the negotiators' home field and depart the negotiators' home field, probably in a huff due to the "war" made upon them by the first negotiator. In such an event it is very difficult for the opponents to return to the negotiators' home field even though a second negotiator will be conducting the negotiations. Because of adverse affects suffered as a result of the first negotiator's "war" antics, the thought of reentering may be too much to ask of the opponents. The site of the negotiations may therefore have to be shifted elsewhere, either to a neutral site or to the opponents' home field in order to make any progress.

This site shifting thus introduces a new element into the negotiations which is not only risky but can also diminish the effect of the "war and peace" technique since the opponents will enjoy considerably more psychological comfort from the shift away from the previous controversial negotiating environment. Furthermore, entry by the second negotiator at the new negotiating site may even be considered by the opponents to represent a new, fresh start into the negotiation apart and away from the "war" waged by the first negotiator, thus nullifying to a great extent the first negotiator's efforts.

## CHAPTER 11

# The "Building Block" Power Negotiating Technique

*Things look better merely by being divided into their parts, since they then seem to surpass a greater number of things than before. The same effect is produced by piling up facts.*

Aristotle

In numerous negotiations, you may find yourself painfully deficient of favorable facts necessary to attain your negotiating objectives. A very good technique to overcome this handicap is for you to parcel out the favorable facts that you possess so that they build on each other and thus appear to be of a greater weight and number. The net result is to increase your negotiating power because it transforms a weak factual position into one that seems much stronger.

### How to Apply the "Building Block" Technique

There are essentially two ways to use the "building block" technique effectively. The first, and the one most often available, is to parcel out the facts over the length of only one negotiating session. Many negotiations last for only one negotiating session and that is why the "building block" technique is most often used in these cases. You relate some of the facts at the beginning of the negotiating session and then carefully parcel out the remaining facts over the length of the session. Contrast that to a situation in which you make known all or essentially all of your favorable facts at or near one time during the negotiating session, thus fully exposing the weakness of your factual position, and the worth of using the "building block" technique can be more fully appreciated.

The second way to effectively use the "building block" technique is to parcel out your favorable facts over several negotiating sessions. This procedure has an added advantage in that the additional sessions in and of themselves tend to lend greater weight to the facts. The cumulative effect of one session piled on top of another session gives the impression of greater importance to your position as you parcel out your facts at each session.

You should tactfully repeat at each new negotiating session the facts related at the previous sessions in addition to parceling out new facts. This lends even greater strength to your position, making it appear to be founded upon a solid base of facts.

### Using the "Roller Coaster" Technique for Added Impact

When parceling out the facts over one negotiating session or over several sessions, it is usually wise to commence the factual presentation with some of those facts that most strongly support your position. Then, go into weaker supportive facts and end, again, with the remaining facts that best support your position. This "roller coaster" technique of beginning on a high point with strong supporting facts, then slipping to a low point and ending, again, at a high point at the conclusion of the negotiation with strong supporting facts will have a great impact upon the opponent. The opponent is more apt to remember and attach significance to first impressions and last impressions rather than to those that occurred in between. This phenomenon is a common human characteristic and is one of the reasons why, for example, knowledgeable moviemakers try to make pictures that begin and end on high points.

# CHAPTER 12

# The "Vinegar and Honey" Power Negotiating Technique

*You must make a habit of thinking in terms of a definite objective.*
John H. Patterson

"Vinegar and honey" situations are frequent occurrences in everyday life. Recently while I was waiting to land in a large, filled to capacity commercial jet, the pilot informed the passengers that because of heavy traffic there would be an hour's delay in landing. Grumbling and angry comments immediately filled the air and most passengers settled down to a long, boring wait. A few minutes later the pilot announced that the delay had been cut to only a half hour. There were sighs of relief among the passengers. About five minutes later the pilot announced that we had been cleared for landing in only a few minutes. The passengers became jubilant. So here we had a situation in which although their airplane was actually late, the passengers were happy.

This technique of initially imparting bad news (the vinegar) and then gradually relieving the bad news with doses of good news (the honey) in order to gain acceptance even though the final news is bad, works wonders in negotiation.

For instance, assume a union wants a 5 percent wage increase. It goes to the bargaining table asking for a 20 percent increase which is, indeed, a heavy dose of vinegar to the company. Slowly, the union retracts its wage demands until eventually it receives its sought-after 5 percent. The company feels good about the final outcome since giving a 5 percent wage increase is preferable any day to giving a 20 percent wage increase. The union, of course, is equally quite satisfied and is really the one who ended up the victor.

### The "Honey" Can Be Varied

The honey being dispensed to sweeten the vinegar need not be directly related to the vinegar. For example, assume the union also asks for shorter working hours, more medical benefits, and more holidays in addition to the 20 percent wage increase. In making these demands, the union anticipates difficult bargaining and hopes to settle eventually for an 8 percent wage increase. As discussions progress, the union gradually and at strategic points, gives in on each of its other demands of shorter working hours, more medical benefits, and more holidays in return for higher wage increases until the union eventually secures a wage increase of 10 percent, but nothing more. The union, of course, has more than accomplished its negotiating objective of at least an 8 percent wage increase. The company also feels good about the outcome due largely to the honey dispensed by the union in the form of giving in on its other demands.

### The Danger to Avoid When Using the "Vinegar and Honey" Technique

In the late airplane example, the passengers were "captives" because there was nothing they could do to alleviate the situation. In most negotiations, however, if the news is too bad or unfavorable, the opponent may merely walk away from the negotiations. In the union vs. company example, the company may have walked out if the union's demands were too great. The net result could have been a strike that would have been costly to both the union and the company. Accordingly, it is very important when using the "vinegar and honey" technique to be certain that the "vinegar" is not so sour that the negotiator is not afforded the opportunity to sweeten it by dispensing the "honey."

The negotiator's judgment as to how strong to make the vinegar is therefore vitally important to the successful use of the technique. It is impossible to overemphasize the value of experience and a keen understanding of human nature. These are two ingredients indispensable to consistent negotiation success. Some opponents can take extremely bad news without blinking an eye. Others are apt to bolt away at even the slightest mention of bad news. Whatever the case, the burden is always upon the negotiator to determine in each individual situation how strong the vinegar should be, and when and how much honey should be dispensed.

Finally, it is important to note that the bad news should always be relevant and necessary to the negotiator's negotiating position. In the union vs. company example, the union must, in fact, really desire all of its original proposals of shorter working hours, more medical benefits, and more holidays in addition to higher wages. In other words, none of the demands should be merely artifical, created simply to gain the sought-after objective of higher wages. What it boils down to is a question of priorities. An increase in wages, in the example, was the primary objective. The other demands, although genuinely desired, were secondary and were sacrificed in order to accomplish the primary objective.

# CHAPTER 13

# The "Conduit" Power Negotiating Technique

*The very essence of all power to influence lies in getting the other person to participate.*

Harry A. Overstreet

One of the most common occurrences in negotiation, particularly in formal negotiation, is to have more than one person working on the opponent's side. Whenever this occurs, the negotiator is afforded the opportunity to use the "conduit" power negotiating technique.

In virtually every negotiation in which there is more than one opponent, only one opponent possesses the authority, either actually or due to a dominant personality, to make all final decisions concerning the negotiation. The opponent who possesses such authority is, of course, the one that the negotiator must reach in order to succeed. For simplicity's sake, let's call the opponent who possesses decision-making authority A and the colleagues of A, Group B.

### When the "Conduit" Technique Should Be Used

If the negotiator has worked diligently but to no avail to sway A, the negotiator should then seriously consider swaying that person through A's negotiating colleagues (Group B). Persistence is essential in negotiation just as it is in most every other endeavor. Once the negotiator has reached a stalemate in using one approach, he or she must adopt another approach rather than give up.

Accordingly, if the negotiator cannot succeed in the negotiation by directly convincing A, the negotiator must then simply alter the approach. The "conduit" technique is frequently a very good technique to switch to.

### How the "Conduit" Technique Works

A conduit is a channel for conveying something. The negotiator turns the thrust of the presentation away from A and directs it instead toward the other opponents, Group B. The negotiator works to convince Group B of the merits of his or her position and encourages Group B to channel its concurring thoughts toward A.

The "conduit" technique is effective largely because it is repetitive. The person possessing the final decision-making authority, A, has heard the substance of the negotiator's position earlier and is now, in essence, hearing the same argument as the negotiator presents it to the other opponents, Group B. The negotiator should take care to vary the wording and order of this second presentation so that it will not be *obviously* repetitive. If the negotiator is obviously repetitive, Group B may not be interested in spending time listening to what they have already heard. They might also be less inclined to agree to it and therefore unwilling to attempt to influence A. The negotiator must also expect that a member of Group B may be unable to convey the negotiator's points with the same force and skill the negotiator applied when they attempt to influence A. This risk, however, must be incurred since the negotiator has already met with a deadend in attempting to convince A directly.

### The More Opponents, the Better

A unique feature of the "conduit" technique is that the more opponents there are to work on, the better the technique usually works. The reason is that the negotiator can direct the approach toward all of the opponents and hope to convert as many as possible toward the negotiator's way of thinking. The odds of success are therefore substantially increased. If, for example, there are four opponents, one of whom possesses final decision-making authority, the negotiator can proceed to work on the remaining three. Assume the negotiator initially converts only one opponent to his way of thinking and then draws out the negotiation. The odds have now increased from four to one when the negotiation began (four unconvinced opponents with the negotiator standing alone) to three to two (the three remaining opponents against the converted opponent and the negotiator). Both the negotiator and the converted opponent (not directly as an advocate but as an ally) then proceed to work on the others and as each one is converted, the negotiator's odds increase. This building effect can add considerable power to the negotiator. I have seen situations in which, as each opponent is converted, the pressure to agree with the negotiator's position becomes so great on the person possessing final decision-making authority that he or she literally agrees to the negotiator's position by default, being unable to withstand the favorable pressure generated by everyone involved in the negotiation including his or her own colleagues.

CHAPTER 14

# The "Silence" Power Negotiating Technique

*Let a fool hold his tongue and he will pass for a sage.*

Publilius Syrus

One of the most important attributes of silence is that it forces the opponent to draw conclusions based largely upon the facts and circumstances of the particular situation. Since a person is normally motivated more by his or her own conclusions than those advanced by others, the "silence" technique is a very effective power negotiating technique.

To illustrate, assume you are attempting to negotiate the purchase of a valuable coin. The opponent knows that you enjoy a fine reputation in dealing with valuable coins and have dealt with coin dealers throughout the world. The opponent who inherited the coin from a relative is not a coin dealer and has no real knowledge of what others may be willing to pay for the coin. The facts are rather typical in negotiation and the item that is the subject matter of the negotiation may consist of virtually any type of personal property or even real estate.

The opponent, because of lack of knowledge, begins the negotiation by probing. The probes are generally disguised since the opponent does not want to tip you off concerning his or her complete lack of knowledge of what the coin would bring if sold in other markets. The opponent therefore casually says, "You know, I could get fifty thousand dollars for this coin if I sold it back east." Assume that fifty thousand dollars is substantially less than you are willing to pay for the coin. Assume also that you have not made any offer for the coin at that point in the negotiation. You would therefore like to establish fifty thousand dollars as the upper price limit. Accordingly, you remain silent, preferring to allow the opponent to conclude from your silence that the coin could, indeed, be sold for fifty thousand dollars back east. The opponent's conclusion arrived at in this manner will motivate the opponent toward your negotiating objective of establishing fifty thousand dollars as the upper limit. Thus you will be able to pay less for the coin than you originally intended to pay. In fact, by pointing out that selling the coin back east would entail additional costs such as commissions and security, you are in a strong position to acquire the coin for less than fifty thousand dollars.

**Use of the "Silence" Technique Requires Strong Self-Control**

There is always a tendency in negotiation for a party, either the negotiator or opponent, to speak out on virtually every proposition advanced by the other side. Frequently, either party may feel that failure to speak out somehow indicates weakness on his or her part, perhaps thinking that by remaining silent the other negotiating side will construe the silence to mean lack of knowledge. This is, as the foregoing illustration of the "silence" technique makes clear, a mistake. Skilled opponents often advance propositions for a variety of reasons (other than for the substance of the proposition), reasons such as attempting to probe as in the foregoing coin example, attempting to confuse, or even attempting to delay. Each of the opponent's propositions should therefore be carefully weighed by the negotiator before he or she decides whether to respond, to remain silent, or to avoid the proposition by tactfully but purposely going on to another phase of the negotiation.

The negotiator should also weigh carefully the opponent's silence to be certain that the opponent is not attempting to use the "silence" technique to draw the negotiator into conclusions the opponent desires the negotiator to make. Too often in negotiation an opponent's silence leads the negotiator to jump to conclusions that will damage his or her position. Rather than jumping to conclusions the negotiator should give due consideration and thought toward discovering the reason for the opponent's silence and a proper strategy and technique to counter it.

So, in the final analysis, the common misconception that negotiators negotiate by ceaseless talking should be put to rest once and for all. Only "fools" talk when they should be listening and contemplating. And if there is doubt as to whether to speak or remain silent, remember Publilius Syrus's declaration quoted above and worthy of requoting here:

Let a fool hold his tongue and he will pass for a sage.

It works that way in negotiation.

# CHAPTER 15
# The "Timely Disclosure" Power Negotiating Technique

*Power is not revealed by striking hard or often, but by striking true.*
Honoré de Balzac

The name of this technique comes from the story of a trial lawyer whose case was going very badly. He was prosecuting a defendant accused of selling syringes used for the injection of dope into the body. The lawyer was perceptive enough to realize that the jury was simply not favorably responding to his side of the case although he had clearly connected the sale of the syringes to the defendant. The problem was that the jury was not convinced that merely selling syringes was that harmful a practice.

Toward the end of the trial the defendant was on the witness stand, and the prosecuting attorney was getting ready to cross-examine him. The prosecuting attorney had assembled in a paper carton a large number of the syringes the young defendant was accused of selling. The carton also contained colored pictures vividly portraying the damage done to the users of the syringes. Many had punctured themselves countless numbers of times with the long needles. As he passed the jury box while carrying this gruesome assembly of items, the bottom of the carton suddenly gave way and the carton's entire contents spilled over the rail into the jury box, some of the items even falling on the jurors' laps.

For a few minutes the court was in a state of confusion as members of the jury helped to pick up some of the spilled items. But as they did, they took a hard look at the long needles and the pictures of the people who had been devastated by the drug. Soon thereafter the jury brought in a verdict of guilty. Although unintentional, the timely disclosure by the prosecuting attorney of the true nature of the apparatuses and the evil purposes for which they were used was more than sufficient to secure a verdict of guilty.

**The Two-Fold Effect of the "Timely Disclosure" Technique**

It is important that you realize that the impact of using the "timely disclosure" technique is two-fold. The initial impact occurs immediately when the disclosure is made. In the trial story, the moment the spill occurred and the jurors could see what the spilled items were, they began to sense the relevancy of the items to the case before them.

The same is true in negotiation. Once the timely disclosure is made, whatever the disclosed item may be, the opponent will immediately begin relating its relevancy to the negotiation. The disclosed item becomes a motivator. It is at this juncture that you must be certain that such motivation is directed toward your negotiating objectives.

The secondary impact of the timely disclosure occurs when the disclosed item is carefully and skillfully woven into your proposals and therefore specifically directed toward your negotiating objectives. In the trial story, this would have been done by the prosecuting attorney during his subsequent cross-examination of the defendant and perhaps other witnesses. In negotiation, the net effect is to convert the item into a powerful negotiating tool.

**Examples of the "Timely Disclosure" Technique in Negotiation**

Any tangible items that can be relevantly used in negotiation are possibilities for use in the "timely disclosure" technique. They can consist of everything from documents (such as financial statements, appraisals, and medical reports that are laid before an opponent) to props, replicas, models, figures on a chalkboard, and even books and magazines. The point is that anything that is relevant to the negotiattion and *can have a sudden, dramatic impact upon an opponent* should be considered a candidate for timely disclosure.

For example, I was representing a client who wished to persuade another to go into a food business venture with him. My client brought with him a miniature replica of the proposed name of the business venture and an attractive logo. These were kept out of my opponent's sight. During the initial stages of the negotiation, a general picture of the proposed business venture was explained. Thereafter, at what was considered a timely place, the replica was suddenly produced and unveiled. Its favorable impact upon my opponent was immediately apparent and, as earlier noted, during this initial period after disclosure my opponent promptly began to sense its relevancy to the subject matter of our discussion.

In order to direct my opponent's initial motivation toward my client's negotiating objective of getting my opponent to enter into a business venture with him, I then, as carefully and skillfully as possible, began specifically tying the replica into the proposed business venture.

### The Best Time to Use the "Timely Disclosure" Technique

Timing in negotiation comes largely with experience. An important element of this experience is a keen knowledge of people. In the trial story, fortunately for the prosecuting attorney, spilling the syringes and pictures occurred at precisely the right time: that is, at the time the defendant was on the witness stand. The jury was able easily to relate the sordid collection of needles and photographs directly to the defendant.

In my business venture negotiation, it was decided that the best time to uncover the replica was after preliminary discussions that were aimed at acquainting my opponent with the general idea involved. Once these discussions had ended, the replica was revealed. The specifics of the business venture could then be related as additional ammunition supportive of the objective the replica was attempting to convey.

In substance, then, there is no ideal time to make a timely disclosure. Rather, once you decide to use the "timely disclosure" technique, you must then decide the point in the negotiation at which to put the technique into operation. This decision can ordinarily be made during the course of preparation prior to the actual discussions. However, you should realize fully that you may very well have to change your time plans because of circumstances developing during the negotiation. You should therefore be fully prepared to scrap any earlier timing plans for making the disclosure and quickly, sometimes during the course of the actual discussions, arrive at a new time for introduction.

**The Greatest Danger in Using the "Timely Disclosure" Technique**

The greatest danger in using the "timely disclosure" technique is that the opponent will fail to *immediately* sense the timely disclosed item's relevancy and connection to the subject matter of the negotiation. When that occurs, any anticipated dramatic impact upon making the disclosure is lost and you must then proceed to connect the disclosed item to the subject matter of the negotiation.

If, in the food business negotiation, for example, when the replica was suddenly disclosed, my opponent had failed to sense its relevancy to the subject matter of the negotiation *immediately* upon its disclosure, I could have lost a material amount of negotiating momentum and thus risked the loss of negotiating power. Consequently, you should take great care to be certain that the item being suddenly disclosed is of such a nature and is disclosed at such a time that there exists little danger that the opponent will fail to sense the relevancy of the disclosed item to the subject matter of the negotiation *as soon as* the timely disclosure is made.

CHAPTER 16

# The "You-Say-You-Don't But-You-Do" Power Negotiating Technique

*One who is in the habit of applying his powers in the right way will carry system into any occupation, and it will help him as much to handle a rope as to write a poem.*

F. M. Crawford

Use of this technique is common even in nonnegotiating situations. Very recently, the host of a television talkshow, before asking his guest a very personal question, prefaced his question by stating: "I don't know if you have ever been asked this before and I don't want to get too personal, but. . . ." The tip-off that the question would be asked was use of the key word "but." There are other key words that are frequently used in lieu of the word "but" such as "however," "nevertheless," and "except." All are designed to facilitate asking the question or making the response and thus to maximize the chances that a response will, indeed, be given.

Often, after use of the key word, additional justification is, or can be, added to further facilitate a response. In the talkshow example, for instance, the host might have said: "I don't know if you have ever been asked this before and I don't want to get too personal *but* there are, I am sure, many of your fans who will be seeing this interview and would like to know." This type of additional lead-in makes it doubly difficult for the person to refrain from responding.

## When the "You-Say-You-Don't-But-You-Do" Technique Works Best

Basic use of this technique in negotiation provides you with a means of broaching delicate or touchy matters that are important to you or, as will be subsequently illustrated, to lead into use of other negotiating techniques, and to do either in such a manner that will not offend the opponent. It is therefore a highly useful technique to facilitate negotiation progress and any technique that does that is one that affords you great negotiating power.

During negotiations, a situation may arise that concerns something very personal to your opponent such as the opponent's feelings or attachment to the subject matter of the negotiation, or maybe even a situation in which the parties have had prior dealings and the opponent feels that you had gotten the best of him or her.

To illustrate, assume that the opponent previously sold you land at a price the opponent originally felt was fair. Later, however, the opponent had second thoughts and concluded that he or she had sold the land for a price that was too low. Now, you and the opponent are negotiating on a different parcel of land. In such a situation the opponent may harbor great resentment toward you and therefore be unwilling to agree on any reasonable price, not because the opponent is not satisfied that the price is fair but rather because the opponent wants to get a much higher price in order to "even the score" for selling the previous parcel of land at a price that the opponent felt was too low.

It is important for you to be aware of this possibility whenever you are negotiating with the same opponent on any new subject matter of negotiation. Once you strongly suspect or are certain that your opponent is harboring resentment caused by a previous negotiation, it is important for you to approach the negotiation very delicately and, in most instances, to regain your opponent's confidence. You might do this by directly getting into the results of the previous negotiation and putting your opponent's concern about the results to rest once and for all.

In order to do this, you might say, "Now look, I don't want to get into our previous negotiation on the other parcel of land because that is fully closed and settled, *but* I thought it might be useful for us to review it briefly." You can then go on to carefully point out why the end result was fair both to the opponent and to you. If this explanation is satisfactory, you have then fully eliminated your opponent's concern and thus opened the door for meaningful negotiations on the property currently under negotiation. The opponent is now in a frame of mind that will, upon your skillful presentation, allow the opponent to be motivated toward your negotiating objectives.

### Leading into Another Negotiating Technique

The "you-say-you-don't-but-you-do" technique is excellent for leading into use of other power negotiating techniques. For example, the "gearshifting" technique (Chapter 17) is a relatively easy technique to lead into with virtually no effort.

To illustrate how you might lead into the "gearshifting" technique, let me draw from an experience. Numerous negotiating sessions had been held concerning the effect of certain court decrees on several of the major issues being negotiated. My opponents' position during the initial negotiating sessions was that the decrees were completely in their client's favor. After several additional sessions, however, my opponents appeared to be weakening on their strong feelings about the effect of the decrees. The negotiations then centered on other issues but, since the issues affected by the decrees were very large and important, I very much wanted to continue to weaken my opponents' feelings about the impact of the decrees by shifting the discussions back to them. I was able to do this smoothly by use of the "you-say-you-don't-but-you-do" technique. I said, in substance, "I know we've previously discussed thoroughly the effect of the decrees and I don't want to rehash old arguments, but. . . ." By use of this technique as a lead-in, I was able to restate on several different occasions over the course of the negotiation my positions on the decrees and to further effectively weaken my opponents' reliance on the decrees.

CHAPTER 17

# The "Gearshifting" Power Negotiating Technique

*Any change . . . must have an end.*

Aristotle

I once rode in a truck over a very hilly road. The driver, a skilled trucker, shifted through the gears beautifully as we climbed and descended each steep hill. He used the gears that he felt would serve best on each climb and descent, shifting quickly and smoothly so that the huge truck lost no momentum as it climbed each hill and gradually slowed as it descended each hill. The truck driver, of course, knew precisely what gears he would shift into. I, on the other hand, had to either anticipate or guess, hoping to come up with the correct answer.

Gearshifting in negotiation, that is, shifting the subject matter of the negotiation from one issue or field to another, if done as smoothly as the truck driver shifted gears, can be a very effective power negotiating technique in negotiations of all kinds and importance. The Russians, for example, in most of their important negotiations such as the Strategic Arms Limitations Talks (SALT), use it, unexpectedly shifting from one subject to another.

### Why the "Gearshifting" Technique Is So Effective

In my truck riding experience, the truck driver knew precisely what gears he would shift into and when he would shift. I had to either anticipate or guess. In negotiation, you enjoy the same advantage as the truck driver when you employ the "gearshifting" technique. You not only know which subject to shift into but also when to shift. The opponent can only anticipate or guess. The usual effect is to throw the opponent off stride, to disorientate the opponent mentally to such an extent that his or her negotiating power is diminished.

**The Type of Negotiation in Which the "Gearshifting" Technique Works Best**

In the SALT talks it was imperative that both the United States and Russia reach an agreement on arms limitations. There was an overriding necessity that both must remain at the bargaining table in spite of the tactics of either. The same overriding necessity is present in a great number of negotiations. The negotiations of company or governmental bodies, such as cities, and unions are good examples. In most negotiations of this sort, the parties must, at some point, eventually reach an agreement even if there is a lockout or a strike. Neither can terminate the negotiations permanently even if they desire to do so. Consequently, if one of the negotiating parties shifts the subject of the negotiations from wages to medical benefits and then to holidays and back again, there is very little the other side can really do but attempt to counter the shifting. The other side cannot, no matter how disagreeable the shifting becomes, permanently break off the negotiations.

In numerous other negotiations it is essential that either one or both negotiating sides reach a successful negotiating conclusion. Perhaps, for instance, one negotiating side is greatly desirous of or needs a particular asset or service that the other negotiating side possesses or has access to. Maybe the asset is a business, patent, parcel of land, or piece of personal property such as a painting, a diamond, or an antique. It might even be an animal like a prize racing or show horse.

It is unwise in most negotiations for you to let your opponent discover that there is an overriding necessity for you to acquire the items that are the subject matter of the negotiation. Once an opponent makes such a discovery, he or she has considerably more negotiating options available to him or her, one of which is use of the gearshifting technique. You should, whenever possible, try to maintain an air of detachment from the items that are the subject matter of the negotiation.

### Gearshifting in Nonessential Negotiations

Negotiations in which an opponent may, at will, terminate the discussions require much more adept use of the gearshifting technique. Obviously, the opponent is not going to sit around and allow you to shift the negotiations from subject to subject or issue to issue at your discretion. If the opponent does allow such a shifting, there is a strong possibility that the opponent considers the subject matter of the negotiation to be essential or, perhaps, the opponent is merely inexperienced or too meek to protest.

In most nonessential negotiations, the best method when employing the gearshifting technique is for you to justify the shift right before making the shift. You know that in most instances the opponent may be forced to go along with the shift if you give sufficient justification for making it.

To illustrate, I was conducting a negotiation that involved a great number and variety of issues. Some of the issues pertained to the valuation of securities and real estate. Other issues concerned interpretations of documents such as trusts. Wishing to employ the "gearshifting" technique in order to maintain positive negotiating momentum, I began shifting from valuation issues to trust interpretation issues and back again, explaining, for example, that since a particular asset valued was a trust asset, it might be wiser to jump to the trust interpretation issue rather than go on to another valuation issue. I continued to suddenly shift from issue to issue in this manner throughout most of the negotiation, always finding ample and completely legitimate justification for the sudden shift. The net result was to put my opponent on the defensive and to increase dramatically my negotiating power.

CHAPTER 18

# The "Self-depreciating" Power Negotiating Technique

*Immense power is acquired by assuring yourself in your secret reveries that you were born to control affairs.*

Andrew Carnegie

A speaker at a large convention, a highly successful salesman, was relating how he achieved his great success. He interspersed comments throughout his talk about how he lacked a formal education beyond grade school and how he even had difficulty reading. The audience loved it. Here was a "rags to riches" man standing before them and, in essence, boasting about his great success. Yet his boasts were tempered with self-depreciating statements about his lack of education that made his audience retain its receptiveness to what he was saying without considering him a braggart and thus without resenting him.

Abraham Lincoln used this technique to save his own life. One day he was confronted by a man who poked a revolver in his face and said: "I swore an oath that if I ever came across an uglier man than myself, I'd shoot him on the spot."

"Shoot me," countered Lincoln, conceding his lack of good looks.

The man retreated, completely "disarmed" by Lincoln's quick, self-depreciating admission.

Hardly anyone likes a "know-it-all" or a braggart. Nor do most people like the thought that they are being subjected to persuasion, *even if they agree with what the persuader is saying.* What self-depreciating statements do is to break down these barriers as they did in the successful salesman's example. They can also be very disarming as they were in the Lincoln episode.

### An Example of Using the Self-depreciating Technique in Negotiation

In a recent negotiation I came across a glaring error made by my opponent. The negotiation was progressing smoothly and I didn't want my opponent to resent my pointing out the error. I, therefore, prefaced my disclosure of the error by remarking, in substance, that I hesitated to apprise anyone of any error because I, too, made similar errors and never really liked to learn of them myself. My opponent immediately became receptive, acknowledging that no one was infallible, and suspecting that he may have erred. When the error was finally disclosed, its impact, having first been tempered by my self-depreciating remarks, was substantially less than might have been the case had I disclosed the error cold, without any prior tempering remarks. By using the "self-depreciating" technique I was thus able to maintain positive negotiating momentum and to favorably motivate my opponent toward my negotiating objectives.

### The Realm of Self-depreciating Remarks Is Broad

Since self-depreciating statements are really remarks aimed at the negotiator, their variety is virtually endless. The statement may consist of an admission of agreement, as in Lincoln's case, or of not being infallible as in my case when seeking to point out an error of my opponent. The statement may be apologetic such as "I'm really sorry to inform you of what I must because I, too, would not like to receive such news." Whatever the approach taken, the central point is that the statement can consist of any remark that tends to reflect upon the negotiator in such a manner as to make the opponent more receptive to what the negotiator is advocating.

### A Danger to Avoid When Using the "Self-depreciating" Technique

There is one limitation to using the "self-depreciating" technique that should be observed. The self-depreciating statement or remark must not be so drastic that it detracts from or harms the negotiator's credibility as either a person or a negotiator. For example, it was one thing for me, in the foregoing experience, to cast doubt upon my own perfection, but quite another if, for instance, I had said that I definitely make frequent errors. In this latter case, my self-depreciating remarks would tend to cast a shadow over my own ability and thus not to motivate others to follow the positions I was advocating.

Admittedly, there is a fine line between casting doubt on one's own judgment in a manner that motivates others and in a manner that turns them away. Nevertheless, it is a line that should not be crossed because, by crossing it, you run the risk of dissipating your negotiating power by failing to motivate your opponents toward your negotiating objectives.

CHAPTER 19

# The "It's-a-Shame-to" Power Negotiating Technique

*Excellence in any art or profession is attained only by hard and persistent work.*

Sir Theodore Martin

In a considerable number of negotiations there is more than one issue to be resolved. Some negotiations, in fact, have dozens of issues. I have handled negotiations in which there were more than 70 issues to be resolved.

Whenever there is more than one issue and some of the issues have been resolved while some remain unresolved you are afforded the opportunity to use the "it's-a-shame-to" technique. The object of the technique is to break the impasse and motivate the opponent toward reaching an agreement on those unresolved issues. The it's-a-shame-to" technique, although it may appear to be "lightweight" in comparison with other power negotiating techniques, is capable of delivering a heavyweight punch when it comes to results. Accordingly, you should be certain that it is a part of your negotiating arsenal.

**When the "It's-a-Shame-to" Technique Works Best**

In most negotiations in which there is more than one issue, some of the issues are more important than others. For example, assume there are six issues to be negotiated. Four are highly important issues and two are, relatively speaking, much less important. Three of the highly important issues have been resolved but an impasse has been reached on the remaining one and also on the two less important issues. In

81

order to motivate the opponent toward reaching an agreement on the remaining issues, you say something like this: "Look, we've resolved three out of the four important issues. *It's a shame to* make that much progress without resolving the remaining issues. Why don't we see if we can resolve them all?" Or, "We've resolved three out of the four important issues and, if we can resolve the fourth important issue, I am sure we can polish off the less important issues. *It's a shame to* give up without giving it a sincere try. Don't you agree?"

It is surprising what results use of this technique will bring. In a large majority of cases the opponent will respond favorably.

Assume, in our example, that after further negotiation the fourth highly important issue is resolved, leaving only the remaining two less important issues unresolved. You merely use the "it's-a-shame-to" technique again to get your opponent to work to resolve the remaining two issues.

### Language of the "It's-a-Shame-to" Technique Can Vary

"It's-a-shame-to" is merely the name given to the technique. Numerous other phrases can be used to accomplish the same results. For example, you might substitute such phrases as: "It's too bad that . . ."; or, "It's unfortunate that . . ."; or even, "We've come this far, let's try to. . . ." The central point is that you use, by effective language, the agreed-upon issues as a basis for motivating your opponent to continue negotiations on any unresolved issues.

When I first began negotiating, I encountered a very capable and experienced negotiator who became visibly upset when we were not able to make any progress on several important issues. "Huh!" he said. "We've come this far and can't finish the job. It's too bad. Huh!" He was using, of course, a variation of the "it's-a-shame-to" technique. With my opponent's lead-out it was only natural to agree that "it was a shame" that we couldn't continue and resolve all of the issues. We did.

### The "It's-a-Shame-to" Technique Can Be
### Effective in Negotiations That Involve Only One Issue

Assume the negotiations are between a company and a union. The sole issue is a wage increase. The union has demanded a 10 percent wage increase. The company has offered a 3 percent increase. After preliminary negotiations the union has lowered its demand to 8 percent and the company has increased its offer to 5 percent. With only a 3 percent difference remaining, either the union or the company might employ the "it's-a-shame-to" technique. The union representative might say, "Look, we have made progress. We're only 3 percent apart. If we don't reach an agreement, the consequences could be a costly strike that will undoubtedly cost both the company and the union much more than a 3 percent difference. *It's a shame to* quit now. Let's see if we can resolve that 3 percent difference." The company's approach could be very similar.

If either the company or the union takes such an approach, it is not a sign that either one of them is weak. On the contrary, the subtleness of the "it's-a-shame-to" technique is that what it attempts to do is to justify fully the reason and need to continue to negotiate without begging, pleading, or similar tactics that do tend to weaken the negotiating position of the party that practices them. Thus the technique actually complements negotiating progress made and says, in essence, "Let's go on to continue to make progress."

CHAPTER 20

# Fear—The Emotional Trigger of Motivation

*Men's actions depend to a great extent upon fear.*

John F. Milburn

No text on the art of the use of power in negotiation would be complete without a discussion of the role of fear in negotiation. To illustrate fear's powerful motivating role in our everyday lives, consider the following true stories.

A couple with six children was having a home built that was supposed to be fully completed by June first. The contractor was running late and made no real effort to get the house completed by the due date. The husband went to the construction site and delivered the contractor a note. The contractor rushed and completed the job. The note read: "After June first, you will have six full-time supervisors under the age of 12."

A kindergarten teacher would frequently go to the public library to pick up a book for each of her 20 students. The librarian complained about the large number of books that the teacher checked out. "Would you prefer that I bring my twenty kindergartners into the library and let them look for their own books?" the teacher asked. Never again did the librarian complain to the teacher.

**The Most Common Fears in Negotiation**

The two most common fears in negotiation are fear of the unknown and fear of loss. All other things being equal, the greater the fear of either, the greater the person experiencing the fear will be motivated.

What you must do is channel this motivation toward your negotiating objectives. When you are able to do this successfully, you have increased your negotiating power tremendously.

**Capitalizing on an Opponent's Fear of the Unknown**

It is familiar knowledge that human beings, since the beginning of time, have feared the unknown. There is no telling how much progress has been delayed because of fear of the unknown. Certainly someone would have ventured forth much sooner than Columbus did to discover America if that someone had not been shackled by fear of what lay in the great ocean beyond what human eyes could see.

It is a relatively simple matter for you to capitalize on your opponent's fear of the unknown and thus increase your negotiating power. For example, assume the negotiation involves recovery for a defective product purchased from the opponent. Assume, too, that the opponent is a department store that sells retail equipment. Further assume that there is sufficent evidence to lead both negotiating parties to believe that the product was truly defective and that the opponent is resisting a full refund, hoping to settle for substantially less. Having met with strong resistance, you advise the opponent that if a full refund is not received within ten days, you will immediately proceed with "steps" that will ensure recovery.

The ten-day deadline is necessary in order to create a state of anxiety within the opponent that will grow greater as the deadline approaches.* Moreover, the opponent will weigh carefully the "steps" that are available to you. Since there is good evidence that the product is truly defective, the variety of "steps" available to you, in the mind of the opponent, will become magnified, looming larger and larger as the ten-day deadline draws nearer and nearer. Will you sue? publicize the defective product and thus hurt the opponent's business? report the product defect to local or federal authorities? Will you do all of these and more? Numerous possibilities may race through the opponent's mind as he or she contemplates the unknowns. Frequently, fear of these unknowns will cause the opponent

---
*See Chapter 7, The "Rainy Day" Power Negotiating Technique.

to cave in and pay the full refund without your taking any further action.

## Concentrating on the Facts or Circumstances That Cause Fear of the Unknown

Once you have discovered an unknown that causes your opponent to fear, you can concentrate on that unknown in order to keep it fresh in your opponent's mind.

This concentration on the unknown should not be done in an "obvious" manner that would enable your opponent to gain the impression that it is being done deliberately. If your opponent gains such an impression, the chances are very good that the opponent will resent the deliberate attempt to play upon that fear. This resentment may cause the opponent to lose all fear. The end result will be to dissipate your negotiating power because of your inability to motivate the opponent via fear, and to increase the opponent's negotiating power as a result of a decrease in your power.

Although this transition seems rather involved, actually it can occur in a matter of seconds, beginning the moment your opponent concludes that you are deliberately playing on his or her fear of the unknown. Your opponent's fear is immediately eliminated in the brief time it takes to become resentful. Hence, great care must be observed whenever you are concentrating on the facts or circumstances that cause fear of the unknown in your opponent.

## Capitalizing on the Opponent's Fear of Loss

In the foregoing example, the "steps" that were referred to in the event full payment is not received in ten days are also important elements that can motivate the opponent toward your negotiating objective. Refunding money paid for the defective product is one thing but having to pay out who knows how much more in attorney fees and court costs in the event the opponent is sued can be instrumental in the opponent's final capitulation to your demands.

Fear of loss is such a common motivating element in negotiation that it behooves you, whenever possible, to pay particularly close attention to both its existence and use. Loss of profit, loss of sought-after purchases such as a business, land, antique, home, or virtually anything that the opponent desires may create sufficient fear to force the opponent to act quickly and pay more than he or she would have had no fear of loss existed.

Take a simple example that occurs virtually every day of the year in one place or another. A couple is buying a home. The salesperson takes them through the house. The wife is thrilled with the kitchen and *in front of the salesperson* tells her husband how much she loves it. The husband does the same, only his strong attachment is to the den and the spacious backyard in which he can barbecue to his heart's content. Both, of course, have tipped off the salesperson to the strong probability that both will fear loss of the house. So the salesperson is alert and capitalizes on that fear by advising both that not only will the house be shown to another couple later that same day, but also that the house is listed under a multiple listing arrangement that means other real estate salespeople may very well be showing the house. Faced with the possibility of losing that wonderful kitchen, den, and backyard, the chances are good that the couple will be motivated by their fear of loss and that they will buy the house, even paying a higher price for it than they would have paid had they no fear of loss.

The moral, of course, is that fear of loss serves as a strong motivator and you should take advantage of it. On the other hand, you should not convey to an opponent, either by word or action, that you want whatever the opponent has, that is, the subject matter of the negotiation. In the foregoing example, if the husband and wife had kept their feelings about the house to themselves and discussed the matter quietly out of earshot of the salesperson, fear of loss may not have been realized because the salesperson would have had no indication that they were so strongly attracted to the property. Similarly, by "leading with your chin," you will substantially increase your opponent's negotiating power, thus decreasing your own negotiating power, whenever you have conveyed to your opponent your strong desire for any item that is the subject matter of the negotiation. Too, you must realize that a skillful opponent will probe frequently during the negotiation to attempt to discover whether you are strongly attracted to the subject matter of the negotiation in order, perhaps, to take advantage of your fear of loss. It is, accordingly, important for you to be constantly on guard for such probes so that you can insulate yourself from being subjected to fear of loss.

### A Further Illustration of Capitalizing on an Opponent's Fear of Loss

I was negotiating a matter with a trial attorney with responsibility for trying the case should a trial become necessary. My client's position was factually very weak but, if it became necessary to go to trial, I was fairly certain that my opponent would have a difficult time establishing proof for one key element of the case. I therefore shifted the discussions away from my client's weak position and concentrated on the fact that the burden of establishing proof rested on my opponent. Since the case was an important one, the opponent with the responsibility to try the case began to display visible edginess at the thought, I concluded, of losing the case because of the difficulty of sustaining burden of proof. I increased my effort toward that aspect of the negotiation even though my opponent frequently sought to shift the discussions back to the factual aspects on which my client's position was weak. Ultimately the case was successfully settled. Fear of loss because of the burden-of-proof issue substantially motivated my opponent toward my negotiating objective even though my client's case was extremely weak.

### Maintaining Flexibility Increases Your Negotiating Power

The experience above focused on an ability to shift the substance of the discussions away from a weak position to a strong one. The ability to accomplish this zig-zag type of negotiating tactic may often become necessary during the course of the negotiation whenever you discover any fear of loss on your opponent's part. It is consequently necessary for you to maintain a flexible stance throughout the entire negotiation in order to be in a position to capitalize on any discovered fears of your opponent. In the experience above, if I had not been in a position to shift with ease from the factual aspects of the negotiation into the burden-of-proof, trial aspects, it would not have been possible to take advantage of my opponent's fear of loss of such an important case. The end result would have been a material decrease in my negotiating power since I would have been forced to proceed with the negotiation on the basis of the weak facts.

CHAPTER 21

# The Negotiator's Language as a Source of Negotiating Power

*Words are the most powerful drug used by mankind.*

Rudyard Kipling

Spoken and written words are the primary instruments of reaching the opponent's main arteries of gaining information, the opponent's senses of hearing and seeing. What influences us most is what we hear and see. Persuasive words, whether they are spoken or written, will therefore motivate the recipient of those words toward the position that the speaker or writer desires just as forcefully as a powerful magnet will attract a tiny pin. Language is therefore a great source of negotiating power.

In virtually every negotiation, whether large, small, important, or trivial, it is, in the final analysis, your spoken and written words that will ultimately be the factor that determines whether or not you accomplish your negotiating objectives. Accordingly, language is what you should spend the greatest portion of your time perfecting so that your effective use of it becomes as habitual as walking, sitting, or eating.

To understand how important language can be in negotiation, consider the following experience. Although there existed numerous other aspects to the negotiation, one aspect concerned the wording of a court opinion. The court opinion provided that the individual "presumably" could add or change beneficiaries of the particular trusts involved in the case. My opponents construed this language to mean that the court held that the individual possessed complete power to change beneficiaries of the trusts. My position was that since the court used the word "presumably" (which means probably rather than certainly), the court never really held that the individual had power to change trust beneficiaries and that that portion of the court opinion was therefore what is legally known as a *dictum*, that is, a remark made by the court that was not necessary to the court's decision. In other words, the court volunteered its observation that the individual "presumably" could change beneficiaries of the trust and didn't really consider whether, in fact, the individual actually could do so since that consideration was not necessary to the court's ultimate decision in the case before it. So there we were, my opponents and I, engaged in a negotiation that involved millions of dollars, discussing the meaning and use of one single word.

## THE NEGOTIATOR'S LANGUAGE SHOULD GET THE OPPONENT'S ATTENTION

*The power of words is immense. A well-chosen word has often sufficed to stop a flying army, to change defeat into victory, and to save an empire.*
                                                                    Emile de Girardin

Recently I read about a woman who telephoned the police to report that a bull was munching on a pine tree in her front yard. Seven officers responded. Within hours the bull had flattened the pine tree, rammed the woman's car and a truck, and driven the officers into hiding. A 13-year-old boy happened by. Sizing up the desperate situation, he picked up a board, went up to the bull, and gave it a good whack on the head. Subdued, the bull was escorted peacefully down the road to its owner. "First," the boy explained, "you have to get the bull's attention."

That is precisely what your language must do—get the opponent's attention. Let's illustrate further how language can grab one's attention. Many years ago while attending a bar association meeting, the speaker, an experienced trial lawyer, was telling about a case that involved a boy who had lost both arms after being run over by a subway train. The case had been tried previously three times by other lawyers, and three times the juries couldn't agree on a verdict. The speaker tried the case a fourth time and when he made his final argument to the jury, in describing the hardships suffered by the boy he merely said, "I had lunch with him and do you know, he eats like a dog." That was it. That was all he said. The language painted such a vivid picture that I still remember it today even though I was not a member of the jury and heard it only at the lecture long after the case was tried. And every time I think of the language, I visualize a boy lapping up his food like a dog. It was attention-grabbing language at its finest. The jury ruled in favor of the boy.

## HOW IT IS SAID IS AS IMPORTANT AS WHAT IS SAID

*For by thy words thou shalt be justified, and by thy words thou shalt be condemned.*
*Matthew 12:37*

An illustration of the importance of how the negotiator speaks can be found in the story about the two students who loved to chew gum in study hall where gum chewing was forbidden. Rather than risk getting caught and being forced to stay after school, both decided to ask for permission from the principal. One asked: "Can I chew gum while I am studying?" Permission was refused. The other student asked: "Can I study while I am chewing gum?" Permission was granted.

A highly successful author once commented that it was easy for him to write. All he had to do was to pay particularly close attention to his use of verbs and adjectives. That is good advice for a negotiator. Verbs, of course, are action words. Some common verbs used in negotiation are paid, wanted, sold, buy, told, said, made, manufactured, earned, worked, printed, marketed, painted, and hired. The list is broad and provides the negotiator with an ample arsenal to choose from when carefully deciding *how* to say what needs to be said. And carefully choose from this arsenal the negotiator should, using verbs that convey both the most action and paint the most vivid picture in the opponent's mind.

The same is true in selecting adjectives. Adjectives are words that modify the nouns or pronouns that are the subjects or objects of a sentence. For example, assume you are attempting to negotiate a lease for office space with an opponent. You say: "The office space is located near fast, convenient elevators, has large, well-situated, picture windows, and overlooks a lush, well-manicured garden." The words "fast" and "convenient" are adjectives nicely describing the mode of access to the space. The words "well-situated" are adjectives clearly denoting that the picture windows are something special. Finally, the words "lush, well-manicured" are adjectives letting the opponent know that by renting the space, he or she will be looking out onto a garden of beauty and not an unkempt jungle or the walls of another building. Even an opponent who is not especially interested in leasing any new space will certainly be tempted to at least look at the proposed space because of your graphic description. And once the opponent is on the premises, you are well on your way to closing the deal. Proper use of adjectives brought to life the nouns, the things that are so material to the leased space, namely, the elevator, the garden and the means of looking at the garden—the large, well-situated, picture windows.

The moral is that you should pick and choose your verbs and adjectives very carefully. They are the best motivators when concisely tied in with the subject matter of the negotiation. They should, when woven in with the remainder of your language, paint a picture that the opponent can clearly and instantly visualize. Once the opponent has visualized the picture that your words have painted, the opponent is bound to be motivated toward your negotiating objectives in a very favorable manner, thus increasing your negotiating power.

## THE NEGOTIATOR'S LANGUAGE SHOULD ENTHUSE—NOT CONFUSE

*A word fitly spoken is like apples of gold in pictures of silver.*

*Proverbs* 25:11

Many years ago I was negotiating the value of a large parcel of real estate. My opponent submitted a lengthy appraisal of the property to substantiate the value he was advocating. I read the appraisal very carefully numerous times and the more I read it, the more thoroughly confused I became. Finally, in sheer desperation, since my opponent was relying so strongly on the appraisal to support his position, I referred him to a particularly confusing paragraph of the appraisal and told him that I had read and reread that paragraph numerous times and still didn't know what it really meant. Then, in all candor, I proposed that if he could tell me what the meaning of that paragraph was, I would agree to his value. Actually, the risk by making such a proposal was not very great. I, an experienced lawyer, was fairly confident that the paragraph in question was undecipherable. My opponent read the paragraph, read it a second, third, and even a fourth time. I had obviously put myself out on a limb and, if he could make sense out of the paragraph and explain it to me, he had a favorable agreement on the value of the land. He even read the paragraph aloud. Like me, however, the more he read it, the more confused he became until he finally threw the appraisal aside to the far corner of his desk and said, "I see what you mean. Let's forget the appraisal and work out the value ourselves."

Confusing language abounds. Consider the following language reputed to be from a court opinion:

> While trial lawyers devote much congitation and intraprofessional discussion to the matter of selecting a proper jury—propriety presumably being equated with fairness and disinterestedness—nevertheless, because of the uncertainty of human reactions to often unknown or unanticipated motivating factors, the entire voir dire procedure is fraught with precariousness as to whether the desired resultant jury will be realized. Character qualities derivable from interrogation are often elusive and the answers to questions may frequently be illusory as a firm basis for any type of challenge.

The entire paragraph *might* be simply stated: "It is highly difficult to select a favorable jury." But the language is so wordy and evasive and contains so many large, colorless words that not only does the reader have difficulty in concentrating on it but also in concluding with any certainty precisely what it really means. Its end result is to confuse—not to enthuse.

Contrast the language in the paragraph with the language employed by the attorney who informed the jury that his armless client "eats like a dog." I would venture to say that if that attorney had, instead, used language similar to the legalistic paragraph, the jury would have undoubtedly failed again to reach a verdict as it had failed to do in three previous trials.

## THE NEGOTIATOR'S LANGUAGE IS THE "VEHICLE" OF NEGOTIATING POWER

*To get your ideas across, use small words, big ideas, and short sentences.*
John H. Patterson

Once while Abraham Lincoln was trying a case in court, his opponent quoted a Latin legal maxim and turned to Lincoln and said: "That is so, is it not, Mr. Lincoln?"

"If that's Latin," replied Lincoln, "you had better call another witness."

Lincoln fully understood the great power of using simple, easy to understand language. He also was a master of brevity. His Gettysburg Address is a lasting testament to that. The Lord's Prayer is another example of powerful ideas simply stated. Both the Gettysburg Address and the Lord's Prayer are excellent examples of the use of simple, concise language concerning big ideas. Both make their points vividly and clearly.

### The Negotiator's Warehouse of Knowledge

The negotiator who has fully prepared for the negotiation has a mind stored with knowledge just like a warehouse filled with merchandise. Language is the vehicle that delivers the message. The more effective the language used, the more efficiently the knowledge is applied.

To further understand how proper use of language is the vehicle of negotiating power, consider what occurred during negotiations between the United States and North Korea concerning the release of the crew of the American ship *Pueblo* that had been captured by North Korea. North Korea insisted that the United States sign a document admitting that the *Pueblo* was a spy ship. In addition, North Korea wanted the United States to publicly apologize for the *Pueblo's* alleged intrusion into North Korean waters and to ensure that no such acts would ever again be committed.

The United States, of course, denied the North Korean allegations and had no intention of signing a document that would be an admission of guilt. The negotiations were long and tedious. Finally, Nicholas Katzenback, then Undersecretary of State, suggested that the United States negotiator, Maj. General Gilbert H. Woodward, ask the North Korean chief negotiator whether the North Koreans would release the *Pueblo* crew if the United States acknowledged "receipt of the crew on a document acceptable" to the North Koreans. This suggestion forced the North Koreans to disclose whether they would release the crew for a signed document other than the one that would incriminate the United States. The end result was to remove the impasse brought about by the United States' refusal to sign the incriminating document submitted by North Korea. This added important momentum to the negotiations that ultimately resulted in the release of the entire crew.

## THE NEGOTIATOR'S LANGUAGE SHOULD FIT THE CIRCUMSTANCES OF THE NEGOTIATION

*It is an excellent rule to be observed in all discussions that men should give soft words and hard arguments.*

Wilkens

Joseph Stalin ruled the Soviet Union for many years. His rein was brutal. One of the reasons he came to power was an effective technique he employed when he spoke. He never abused an opponent nor used violent language. Rather, he used soft words but always combined them with hard, incisive arguments.

Not only should the tone of the words fit the occasion but so should the words themselves. For example, recently while in a restaurant, a customer sitting next to me asked the waitress what the entrée was for the day. It was a busy restaurant and very informal. The waitress became visibly confused. The customer was not communicating on the proper wavelength. Use of the word "entrée" did not fit the occasion in that type of restaurant.

In negotiation, if you use a word or phrase that does not fit the occasion, your opponent may become confused. When that occurs you will be stifling negotiating momentum and thus dissipating your negotiating power. Loss of power can occur even if your opponent's confusion is momentary because it is almost always more difficult to regain momentum once it has been stifled or lost than to maintain it.

## THE NEGOTIATOR SHOULD AVOID WORDS THAT TEND TO POLARIZE THE OPPONENT'S THINKING

*Mastery of language affords remarkable power.*

Franz Fanon

Examples of commonly used words that tend to polarize an opponent's thinking are "millionaire," "playboy," "politician," "housewife," "ex-convict," "athlete," "industrialist," "daredevil," "actor," "tightfisted," "hardnosed," and even "genius." Each of these words has the power to polarize.

The primary reason why such words should be avoided in most negotiations is that they call forth stereotypic images, and also prejudices concerning those images, in the opponent's mind. Frequently these images may not forward the aim sought by the negotiator. In addition, by using such words, the negotiator has failed to paint the type of vivid picture necessary to persuade the opponent to accept the negotiator's point of view. The end result is that the negotiator's negotiating power is diminished.

It is important to note that words that tend to polarize a person's thinking differ from one negotiation to the next. For example, assume that you, the negotiator, represent the seller of a large parcel of land. You know that your opponent, the prospective purchaser, is fully aware of the complete details of the land and that the asking price for the land is truly a "bargain." Your use of the word "bargain" would not be polarizing in such circumstances and would not materially detract from your negotiating power since you know that the chances are very good that your opponent will relate your use of the word to the opponent's knowledge of the complete details of the land that make it a good deal.

If, on the other hand, the opponent had no knowledge, or only a spotty knowledge, of the details of the land that make the offered price truly a bargain, your use of the word "bargain" in such a case could materially detract from your negotiating power since the opponent may think that, by using the word "bargain," you are attempting to influence the opponent into believing that a bargain exists when, in fact, it does not exist. It would not be uncommon when such a situation develops for an opponent to ask you why the price is such a "bargain." When that occurs, it is a sure sign that your use of the word "bargain" was a mistake and, unless you quickly recover by pointing out clearly why the price of the land is being offered at a price that is truly a bargain, you will be running the risk that your opponent will not pay the asked price.

Now one may ask, "Why, if the price of the land is being offered at a bargain, isn't there always another buyer?" In some cases there may be. In others, however, there may not. For example, the land might be so desirable that the ultimate price may be up in the hundreds of thousands or even millions of dollars so that there is a limited number of purchasers that can afford the price, even though the land is a bargain. There could be a variety of other circumstances. Perhaps the purchaser may be one of a few that is able to pay cash for the property or the seller may have already incurred considerable expenses with the property or for other reasons must sell the property very soon. The point is that the burden is upon you to accomplish your negotiating objectives with *this* purchaser and not to struggle through the negotiation feeling that sooner or later someone will pay the stated price in spite of how unskillfully you conduct yourself.

## THE LANGUAGE USED NEED NOT FOLLOW FORMAL GRAMMATICAL RULES

> *Such as thy words are, such will thine affections be esteemed: and such as thine affections, will be thy deeds.*
> 
> Socrates

Persuasive language that gets an opponent's attention, whether spoken or written, need not follow the formal guidelines taught to us in school. Nor must the words be long, or scholarly. You are trying to communicate with, and not necessarily to impress your opponent. Your words should therefore be designed to accomplish one and only one objective—to communicate in the most effective manner possible. This means that you should choose the language you feel will not only be fully understood by your opponent but also the language you feel will best motivate your opponent toward your negotiating objectives.

To illustrate, many highly successful songs use language that may not conform to the rules taught in the classroom but communicate, nevertheless, just as effectively. The lyrics from many top hits may not follow formal grammatical rules but they get their message across and are therefore very effective communication.

### You Should Speak Your Opponent's Language

Flexibility is unquestionably a good policy. If, for instance, your opponent is highly educated and uses "highbrow" language, you may decide to use similar language the better to communicate. If, on the other hand, your opponent perfers to use common, everyday street language, you could decide to use the same type of language in order to most effectively communicate. What you should do in essence, is tailor your language to suit your opponent.

You should, during the course of the negotiation, be particularly alert to your opponent's language and adjust your own language to match your opponent's language. Speaking your opponent's language is the most effective way to communicate. Once there is a bridge of effective communication existing between you and your opponent, you have materially increased your chances of motivating your opponent toward your negotiating objectives and thus have increased your negotiating power.

## THE NEGOTIATOR'S LANGUAGE SHOULD BE SINCERE

*Words are the voice of the heart.*

Confucius

There are literally volumes written on the need to think positively. One of the first principles of good sales ability is to believe in the product. That belief will be translated into a positive attitude that will greatly influence others and motivate them to buy the product. The same principle is applicable to negotiation. If you, the negotiator, truly believe in the positions that you advocate, your belief will be translated into positive, sincere language and your sincerity will be detected by your opponent. There is no way it can work otherwise. All of your actions—the way you walk, sit, smile, and move about—will reflect that air of believability and sincerity.

The contrary, of course, is also true. It doesn't take very long for most perceptive persons to detect lack of sincerity on another's part.

And when lack of sincerity is evident, there is little question that your opponent will not be favorably motivated toward your negotiating objectives. Your negotiating power is thus dissipated, perhaps to such an extent that your opponent will not be influenced by you even when you are trying to reflect sincerity. The moral is for you to be certain that the language you use reflects sincerity not only at the beginning of but also throughout the entire negotiation.

## REAPING THE BENEFITS OF THE "POWER OF THE PEN" IS ESSENTIAL TO CONSISTENT NEGOTIATION SUCCESS

*Writing, when properly managed, is but a different name for conversation.*
Laurence Sterne

One of the advantages the written word has over the spoken word is that it can be amended. After writing, you can add and prune until the product that emerges will be the perfect agent to accomplish your sought-after objectives.

Years ago I had the opportunity to see some of the original work of Jack London, the renowned American author. London wrote with an ink pen. There were numerous places in his manuscripts at which he had scratched out a word and inserted another which he thought was better. He scratched out that word and added still a better word. This process of pruning and striving to find the precise word or phrase is what most good authors go through before settling on a final product. It is precisely what you, the negotiator, should do before placing the written work—a letter, contract, appraisal, memorandum, or even a note written on a scrap of paper—in the hands of your opponent.

There are several significant reasons for the need for this precision in writing. Since language is such an important source of negotiating power, the same care and precision should be used with the written word as is used with the spoken word. Second, the written word is more restrictive than the spoken word. Once the opponent has possession of the writing it is much more difficult for you to withdraw what has been written even if it turns out that the words offend the opponent or otherwise result in a detriment to your negotiating position.

The risks of written material being detrimental to your position are much greater when you are not the author of the writing. This may frequently be the case. If the subject matter of the negotiation, for example, requires a written appraisal or a financial report, the chances are good that someone other than you will write the actual report. In such cases, it is strongly recommended that you review a draft of the report, not to change its substance, but to make absolutely certain that it is written clearly and persuasively. As earlier related in this section on language, how something is said is just as important as what is said.

**Writings That Cause the Greatest Loss of Negotiating Power**

Dictating machines are great. They save time and, in many instances, money. But they also can diminish a considerable amount of negotiating power if they are not properly used. Letters are the biggest culprit. A common practice is to dictate a letter, to make changes in the course of dictation, then to sign the typed letter. For routine letters, this practice is fine. For letters that concern important negotiations, the practice often results in disaster. In fact, skilled negotiators are usually adept at finding language in their opponent's letters and using it against their opponent, thus substantially increasing the negotiators' negotiating power.

In order to avoid this potential danger and reduce the risk of dissipating your own negotiating power, you should have only drafts typed from dictated letters. You should carefully scrutinize these drafts to be absolutely certain they state precisely what you intend them to state. Following such a procedure will assist in ensuring that your letters will increase your negotiating power rather than decrease it, since the written language itself will serve to favorably motivate your opponent toward your negotiating objectives rather than to provide the opponent with ammunition that can be used against you.

Another good practice is to have a cooling-off period between the time the letter or other document is drafted and the time it is finalized and sent to the opponent. Whenever possible, this cooling-off period should last at least overnight. The draft of the document can be reread in the morning when your mind is fresh. It is surprising how many flaws can be discovered in the draft and, on occasion, you even wonder when you reread the draft whether you were really capable of doing such a poor job the previous day. If, on the other hand, you are pleased with the morning reading, you can be more assured that it is a good document that will strengthen your negotiating power rather than weaken it.

CHAPTER 22

# The Step Method of Using Negotiating Power

*In all negotiations of difficulty, a man may not look to sow and reap at once; but must prepare business and so ripen it by degrees.*

Francis Bacon

Too often, the use of power is visualized as a quick, telling blow that destroys an opponent and leads to more or less instant victory. Actually, it is common to have a negotiation encompass a great number of negotiating sessions over a long period of time. To the skilled negotiator such an approach is not always accidental. In fact, the negotiator may deliberately proceed on a step-by-step basis for a variety of reasons.

**Easing the Degree of Negotiating Difficulty**

On numerous occasions a negotiation may be highly difficult because of a combination of factors such as complex issues and poor or strained relationships between the negotiating parties. Its outcome could have grave or important effects not only on the negotiating parties but also indirectly on the public. An example of a negotiation that encompassed virtually all of these factors were the peace talks between Egypt and Israel. The outcome affected not only the countries of Egypt and Israel but also all of the Middle East and, indeed, the entire world. Because of the importance of oil to the world's economy and because of the potential for a flare-up that could ignite a devastating world war, the implications of the peace talks were enormous.

105

Yet, whatever may be the handicaps, the burden still remains upon the negotiator to arrive at a successful conclusion to the negotiations. In such instances it is normally wise for the negotiator to consider having more than one negotiating session in order to ease the degree of difficulty. A negotiator can use the early sessions to develop a greater rapport with an opponent and to break down the complexity of issues progressively, step by step in each session. This may be an ideal way to overcome the degree of difficulty.

You as negotiator should always bear in mind that the burden is upon you to be certain that your opponent fully understands your position on every issue. Sometimes an opponent may not specifically indicate a lack of understanding. Maybe the opponent is reluctant to admit ignorance because of pride or insecurity. It is therefore important that you be very alert to the possibility that your opponent lacks understanding. You can usually detect this by observing your opponent's attitude and by testing your opponent at various stages of the negotiation. If, for instance, your opponent fails to reply to a question which ordinarily would call for a response, the chances are good that this failure to reply may be due to a lack of understanding.

When you commence any negotiation that you either know or have strong reason to suspect will be difficult, you should consider carefully whether more than one negotiating session is necessary. Often, too, negotiations that appear to be relatively simple turn out to be quite complex during the initial negotiating session. This may occur because new, unsuspected matters are introduced by the opponent, matters occur suddenly that affect both negotiating parties, or the opponent makes even greater demands than were originally anticipated. All of these potential occurrences underscore your need to maintain flexibility. You must be fully able to extend the negotiations over more than one period so that the occurrence of any of these or other events will not place you at a disadvantage and cause you to sacrifice any negotiating power.

### The "Perfect Ending" Technique

Since Hollywood began a formula that has been used successfully in countless movies is that the hero, in the end, either gets the girl or dies bravely. This perfect ending theme has sold many, many millions of tickets at the box office and will contine to do so.

You can draw from this perfect ending theme in conjunction with using the step method of exerting negotiating power. For example, assume the negotiation involves highly controversial aspects. When it does, you should consider whether or not to have more than one negotiating session in order to deal with the highly controversial aspects of the negotiation during the earlier sessions. Thereafter, you can concentrate on the remaining noncontroversial aspects at the later or final negotiating session in order to effectuate the "perfect ending."

The same is true in situations in which there are many glaring weak spots in your position. You get the weak spots on the negotiating table at the initial negotiating sessions and use the later or last session to dwell on your strong points. This is an important reason why you should carefully gauge each of your strengths and weaknesses. By so doing you are able to decide upon a manner of dealing with each. You will be able to formulate your strategy early, thus placing yourself in a more favorable position to take advantage of using more than one negotiating session when you feel it is wise to do so.

When adopting this step-method approach, it is virtually impossible, of course, to determine the precise number of negotiating sessions that may be necessary to get the opponent in the frame of mind to be fully receptive to your final use of the strongest part of your case. This is where experience and postnegotiation analysis really pay off. There is, indeed, no substitute for experience. Equally important, however, is the necessity to fully analyze every negotiation in an objective manner and to draw from each one those aspects that were handled well in order to retain and improve upon those aspects that were handled poorly.

CHAPTER 23
# How Mental Practice Increases Negotiating Power

*The trained mind is the most powerful instrument in the whole world.*
Charles W. Cole

Josef Hofmann, the renowned concert pianist, was leaning back in his seat with his eyes closed while on a train bound for a city in which he was to give his next concert. A friend asked, "Are you sleeping?"

"No," replied Hofmann, "I'm practicing."

Doris Day, one of America's most popular actors, used the same technique to increase her performing abilities. She said:

> I would drag myself home at night, too tired to move another step, but I kept practicing—in my head. . . . I could rehearse a dance routine in my head, watching myself perform, and that did me almost as much good as getting up on my feet and doing it. I rehearsed songs that way too. Not just lyrics, but the actual rendition of the song, the phrasing, breathing, all of it, without singing a note.*

## Mental versus Physical Practice

It has been firmly established that not only will proper mental practice enhance one's ability but also can be even superior to practicing by doing the actual act. The basic reason is that the subconscious mind and the nervous system cannot distinguish between the experience of actually performing an act and the identical experience

---
* *Doris Day* by A. E. Hotchner. New York: Morrow, 1976, p. 146.

conceived in the mind. That is why Josef Hofmann could effectively rehearse without actually touching a piano and Doris Day could practice without actually stepping on a dance floor or singing a note.

The full import of this phenomenon in relation to negotiation becomes apparent when one realizes the importance of the vast amount of preparation many negotiations entail and, even more importantly, that there is literally no opportunity for a "dress rehearsal" in the presence of the actual opponent before the real negotiations begin. Mental practice may serve the same function and bring the same result. In fact, even in those negotiations most persons encounter in the course of their lives, such as buying or remodeling a home, buying a car, or even dealing with someone to fix an appliance that never seems to work, a brief amount of mental practice, if done properly, can easily enhance your negotiating power and make the difference between accomplishing your negotiating objective or failing.

**What Mental Practice Really Means**

Thinking about the results of a matter may improve one's memory of that matter but will not be a substitute for actual practice. For example, let's say you are a young person aspiring to become a top quarterback. You will not successfully assist in accomplishing your objective merely by imagining yourself meeting the press, accepting trophies for a great season, or even by visualizing yourself on the cover of national sport magazines and in all of the newspapers. The most such daydreams can accomplish is to fire you with the desire to become an outstanding quarterback. But desire without ability is like a flag without a pole—you have no chance of even getting the flag flying, let alone keeping it there.

In order to substitute mental practice for physical practice, you must actually visualize yourself going through all the acts that a quarterback must go through, from the time you enter the huddle to the time you let loose the ball. You should actually see yourself looking at your teammates and calling the play, getting up behind the center, taking the snap of the ball, and either passing or handing it off to a runner. This actual visualization is, in many instances, even better than physically doing the same acts because the mental visualization will ordinarily be letter perfect whereas the actual performance of the acts is often filled with errors that can lead to bad habits or discouragement. The perfect visualization, on the other hand, will eliminate or head off any potential bad habits. You will later go through the acts physically that you have perfectly imagined and will be more apt to do physically what your mind and nervous system have practiced and have had engrained in them *in the same perfect manner.*

It follows from our football example that as a negotiator you should mentally visualize yourself going through each detail of the negotiation as if you and your opponent were actually sitting down together. This means that you can actually visualize your opponent in the environment in which the negotiation is expected to be held and even think of the actual words and the power negotiating techniques you will use. If you have mentally conceived of yourself using flawless techniques, the chances are very good that you will perform equally as well when you use them during the actual negotiation. You may even visualize your opponent's reaction to the techniques being used and thereby be able to eliminate rough spots in the actual negotiation.

In fact, when preparing for important negotiations, I frequently and actually sit in the chair I expect my opponent to occupy (in an environment I have selected), close my eyes, and assume the role of my opponent, visualizing myself as the negotiator using the techniques and even making offers and counteroffers. Through this method I am able to eliminate to a great extent faulty techniques or unreasonable offers or counteroffers.

## One Great Danger of Utilizing Mental Practice

Since the mind and nervous system cannot distinguish between the actual experience and the same experience mentally conceived, any mental conceptions based upon faulty premises such as errors of fact, hearsay, or faulty use of techniques will be translated into the same mistakes during the actual acts. Referring back to our football example, if you have visualized yourself using an incorrect hand position for receiving the ball from the center or for throwing the ball, your mind will register that improper grip and the chances are very good that you will use the same improper grip when you are actually receiving or throwing the ball on the practice field or in the game. If Doris Day had mistakenly visualized the wrong lyric when she mentally practiced her songs, the chances are very strong that she would sing the wrong lyric when the time came for her to actually sing.

For this reason, it is highly important that you be absolutely certain that what you visualize when you practice mentally is accurately conceived so that you do not go into the negotiation handicapped. A negotiating technique improperly executed mentally and, as a consequence, improperly executed during the actual negotiation will obviously work to your detriment and thus dissipate your negotiating power. The same is true of any other aspect of the negotiation that you have incorrectly practiced mentally.

CHAPTER 24

# Motivating an Opponent through Your Facial Expressions

*A flicker of the eye lids, a wrinkle of the brow or a twist of the lips, all are so revealing to the trained eye.*

Anonymous

The most important point to remember about facial expressions is that they "talk" just as effectively as the spoken word. It is therefore essential that your facial expressions be compatible with the impressions that you *desire* to convey to your opponent.

To illustrate, let's consider the experience of James Ling, chief builder of LTV Corporation, a large, multimillion dollar company. Ling was attempting to sell a company and expected the purchaser to make an opening bid in the range of $60 to $65 million. The parties were sitting across the table from each other. After some brief comments, the prospective purchaser announced that his company was willing to pay $90 million for Ling's company.

Ling continues:

> I sat there trying to organize my thoughts, because here I am with an opening bid maybe $30 million higher than I had expected it to be.
>
> ... My face was a complete mask ... it showed no expression of any kind.
>
> ... Then I suggested that [my associates] and I should caucus in [my associates'] office and [the purchaser] should remain at my conference table.
>
> I did not smile as we went through the reception area.... *

---

*Ling: The Rise and Fall of a Texas Titan* by Stanley Brown. New York: Atheneum, 1972, p. 229.

A smile (which would have been the normal reaction for a person receiving an offer $30 million higher than anticipated) from Ling *or any of his associates* under the foregoing circumstances could have endangered the entire transaction and caused the prospective purchaser to withdraw his offer before Ling and his associates had an opportunity to caucus. A smile from Ling or any of his associates would have said just as effectively as if the words had been spoken, "Your offer is much higher than we anticipated."

But Ling and his associates remained impassive, and conveyed no information to the prospective purchaser which was exactly what Ling *desired* to convey. He wanted to make it appear as if the offer was truly too low—so low, in fact, that he and his associates had to call for a caucus to decide whether to accept or reject the offer.

**Why Facial Expressions Are So Revealing**

People are accustomed to gaining knowledge and drawing conclusions from that knowledge merely by watching the faces of others. A smile usually indicates happiness; a frown, displeasure. An expression of pain doesn't even have to be described here. Almost everyone can tell at a glance when another is in pain just by looking at the other person's contorted face. In most cases the conclusions drawn that are based upon the person's facial expressions may be correct. In negotiation, as the Ling experience illustrates, this may not necessarily be the case. Skilled negotiators are fully aware of the fact that facial expressions "talk" just as plainly and persuasively as the spoken word and they therefore consciously make certain that their facial expressions convey only the impressions that they wish to convey to their opponents.

**Warn Your Associates to Control Their Facial Expressions**

In the Ling Story, emphasis was placed on the fact that Ling's associates present at the negotiation remained just as impassive as Ling did when the high offer was made, and they did this for a very important reason. In most cases, opponents will think that any of the negotiator's associates share completely in every bit of knowledge about the negotiation that the negotiator possesses even though the associates may not, indeed, possess such knowledge. Hence, the acts of the associates will be equated with the acts of the negotiator. In other words, if any of Ling's associates present at the negotiation smiled or indicated pleasure at hearing an offer $30 million higher than expected, their reaction would have been attributed by the opponent to Ling and could have seriously jeopardized the transaction.

To further illustrate, several years ago during the course of a negotiation, I was accompanied at the negotiation by a representative of my client. The negotiations progressed very well and, as time wore on, my three opponents suddenly announced that they were going to concede a major point. Their concession, in essence, meant that it would be relatively easy for us to successfully conclude the negotiation. At announcement of the concession, a smile immediately appeared upon my client's representative's face. The adverse reaction from all three opponents was immediate. They attempted to back off from the concession. Fortunately, we were able to fully recover and hold them to their concession.

Finally we left the negotiation room. I knew that our opponents could watch us from the window of their office once we were outside the building. I therefore quietly advised my client's representative as we were about to leave the building to maintain a completely impassive facial expression and not to speak to me until we were completely out of our opponents' sight even though we were both very pleased with the outcome and had, therefore, ample reason to wear broad smiles.

CHAPTER **25**

# Making Assumptions to Increase Negotiating Power

*Most powerful is he who has himself in his own power.*

Seneca

Making an assumption is taking something for granted. It is supposing something to be a fact even though there is no definite proof that the something did or will occur or does or will exist. For example, if you can see only the top part of a traffic light but not the street, you can assume that when the light turns green cars will move on the street even though you cannot see the cars. You base your assumption on your knowledge that cars are allowed to move freely on green lights.

But what if there were no cars on the street on which the light is located or what if the street were blocked off to traffic for street repairs? In either of these instances, your assumption that cars will be moving when the light turns green would be incorrect. Making assumptions, therefore, always entails some degree of risk because to assume the existence of a fact or event without definite proof means you can never be certain that the assumed fact or event did or will take place.

**How Making Correct Assumptions Increases Negotiating Power**

During the course of a complicated negotiation lasting several years and entailing numerous sessions, a court decision was rendered that, although not directly related to the negotiation, had an important

118    Chapter 25

indirect impact. Knowing that I would be negotiating soon and that my opponents were fully aware of the court decision, it was important for me to very carefully analyze the decision and to make accurate assumptions based upon what I felt would be the ultimate impact of the court decision. After a careful analysis, I concluded that the court decision would greatly influence my opponents toward my position. I therefore prepared my negotiation strategy on that basis, making assumptions consistent with that conclusion. One assumption I made, for example, was that my opponents would attack the court decision very early and forcefully at our next negotiating session in order to attempt to weaken its impact and my reliance upon it. I therefore prepared to rebut such an attack. At the next negotiating session the attack I assumed would come did come and, as a result of my correct conclusion as to the effect of the court decision and my assumption that my opponents would attempt to strongly attack the decision and weaken my reliance upon it, I was able to thwart my opponents' attack and gain substantial concessions.

My negotiating power, as a result of my correct assumptions, was substantially increased because I was able to go into the negotiation with fully developed strategies. My only remaining task was to implement those strategies once I was certain that my assumptions were correct. Contrast that to a situation in which I would have had to create strategies and implement them during the negotiation without the benefit of prior preparation and it is easy to see the great value of making correct assumptions and how those assumptions can be tremendously beneficial in assisting a negotiator in attaining negotiating objectives.

**A Tip to Assist You in Making Accurate Assumptions**

There is no foolproof method to ensure that all of your assumptions will be accurate. Experience, of course, will greatly increase accuracy. Even if you are experienced, however, it is important that you remain flexible during the negotiation so that if you discover that one of your assumptions is inaccurate you can quickly act to correct the situation without any material harm to your negotiating position.

A good way to increase the chances of making accurate assumptions is to be certain that assumptions are based upon the opponents themselves rather than upon the issues involved in the negotiation or any other extraneous matters. The reason is that, irrespective of the issues involved in the negotiation and any extraneous matters, it is the opponents who will, in the final analysis, be making the decisions affecting those issues. Hence, making assumptions based upon what those particular opponents will do is the safest way to arrive at reasonably accurate assumptions.

Consider the following example. Since Babe Ruth was a man and hit 60 home runs in one season, it can be assumed that any man can hit 60 home runs in one season. While it may seem logical, this assumption is patently incorrect. The reason the assumption is incorrect is that it takes the facts about a particular man and generalizes them to all men. (It must be pointed out that correct assumptions do not necessarily have to be logical. On the contrary, since most assumptions involve people in some way or another, and because people can be and often are quite illogical, logic and assumptions are, at best, distant cousins.)

Can we then say that since Babe Ruth was a man and hit 60 home runs in a season, it can be assumed that all men can play baseball? The assumption is, of course, still inaccurate because it is still concerned with men in general. Not all men *can* play baseball, as we know.

Finally, can we say that since Babe Ruth was a man and hit 60 home runs in one season, it can be assumed that Babe Ruth was a baseball player? Here we are entirely correct in our assumption because the assumption pertains only to Babe Ruth and not to all men in general. Indeed, Babe Ruth was a baseball player. When the knowledge that a man hit 60 home runs is combined with a little knowledge of the game of baseball, the assumption that whoever accomplished that feat was an excellent baseball player would be highly accurate even if the person making the assumption never heard of Babe Ruth.

Similarly, in my personal experience with the court decision, my assumption as to what my opponents would do as a result of the court decision was based strictly on my knowledge of them since they were the ones who would be making the decisions that affected the negotiating issues. If instead, I had made assumptions based on the effect of the court decision on the issues, the chances are great that my assumptions would have been incorrect.

### Assumptions Are Never Conclusive until They Are Verified

In the court decision experience above, during the initial part of the negotiation I remained alert to detect whether my assumptions concerning the effect of the court decision upon my opponents were correct. Obviously, proceeding with negotiating strategies based on incorrect assumptions can result in loss of substantial negotiating power.

### Facts Are the Most Reliable Bases on Which to Make Assumptions

To return to the traffic light example, anyone making the assumption that cars were moving merely because the light turned green was painfully lacking in facts. All that was known factually was that the light was green and that cars are legally allowed to go on a green light. With only those facts to support it, the assumption that cars were actually moving entails considerable risk of being wrong. If we added the fact that the sounds of traffic are heard coming from the vicinity of the green light, this would increase considerably the *possibility* that the assumption that cars were moving was correct. The essential point is that facts are the only reliable bases on which to make assumptions, and the more facts we have available, the greater the likelihood of our making accurate assumptions.

To further illustrate the importance of using facts to make accurate assumptions and the tremendous power such assumptions can afford the negotiator, let's assume a company's earnings have decreased for three consecutive years (Fact A) under the same management (Fact B) with no new marketing outlets or new products (Fact C). It therefore can be assumed that earnings will decrease next year, all other things being equal. This can be an extremely important assumption if, for example, you are negotiating an employment contract for a new key employee. If your assumption is correct, the corporation badly needs the new talent. You can therefore feel reasonably assured that your demands can go much higher than they could if the corporation were healthy and not in dire need of new leadership.

### Anticipating Assumptions to Increase Negotiating Power

If you represented the corporation in the example above, it would be well for you to anticipate that your negotiating opponent will make the assumption that next year's earnings will also be negative and that your opponent will therefore make high employment demands.

You can move to equalize the effects of this assumption and thus increase your negotiating power by such means as letting your opponent know that there are others being considered for the position (assuming there are). Or you might say that the prospective employee could gain tremendously in prestige by turning the company around into an earnings growth position thus making your opponent realize that the potential rewards for taking the job entail much more than mere monetary rewards.

## Making Assumptions Based upon Assumptions

The likelihood that assumptions based upon other assumptions will be inaccurate is great. Assumptions themselves, although based on facts, are not themselves factual. To base an assumption upon another assumption is therefore as risky as building a house on sand.

To illustrate, in the corporate employment situation in which it was assumed that next year's earnings would decrease, a further assumption based upon that assumption can be made that as a result of next year's decrease in earnings the corporation will be unable to pay maturing debt and will default to its creditors. This assumption based upon an assumption, although a possibility, is obviously much riskier than the original assumption for a variety of reasons. For one thing, there is nothing factual to support it. The company may have ample cash reserves to meet any maturing debt or the company may even have no debt maturing in the foreseeable future. If the corporation's financial statements could be obtained and if they disclosed that there will be considerable debt maturing at the end of the next year with no appreciable cash held by the company, the assumption that the company will be unable to meet maturing debt becomes much more apt to be accurate. Now that facts have been added to support the assumption, however, it no longer is a bare assumption based upon an assumption but is, rather, a normal assumption based upon existing facts which increase greatly its chances of being an accurate assumption.

## The Negotiator Should Be Aware of Opponents Who Anticipate the Negotiator's Assumptions

Skillful opponents know that negotiators will be formulating negotiating strategy partly by use of assumptions, and that facts are what the assumptions will be based on. The opponent may therefore act on occasion in an unexplainable manner in order to attempt to make the negotiator conclude that the negotiator's assumptions are incorrect. For example, assume that a corporate merger is being negotiated and the opponent who represents the company is devoting much attention to a new company product and how that product will greatly enhance future company sales and income. The negotiator who represents the purchaser has already considered the new product in an analysis of the company's worth. The negotiator feels that the product is not *that* good and that it will have no appreciable effect upon either sales or income. It is incumbent upon the negotiator to therefore decide very early whether the opponent (1) is ignorant of the true situation regarding the new product, (2) is merely trying to run up the purchase price, (3) possesses new information about the product that increases the product's potential, (4) is trying to divert the negotiator's attention from more important aspects of the negotiation, or (5) is attempting to magnify the potential of the new product in order to get the negotiator to alter negotiating strategy since the opponent has strong reason to believe that the negotiator has fully considered the new product and has formulated negotiating strategy based upon assumptions made about the new product. All five of the above are real possibilities and if (5) is correct, it is important for the negotiator to discover that as early as possible in order to be able to decide whether to, in essence, disregard the opponent's build-up of the new product and to continue to use the strategy formulated on the assumption that the new product is not that good and will have no appreciable effect upon either future sales or income.

CHAPTER 26

# Nonverbal Forms of Negotiating Power

*Certainly that striking appearance was half the secret of [Daniel Webster's] power....*

John F. Kennedy in *Profiles in Courage*

If an unshaven doctor with uncombed hair, wearing a torn and dirty coat, approached a man and asked him to open his mouth and say "ah," the man might bolt away in fear of his health. If a person *posing as a doctor,* dressed in a medical frock, clean shaven, hair neatly combed and gray at the temples, and a stethoscope dangling from his neck, approached the same man, chances are very good that the man would respond to any reasonable request and would not even ask the fake doctor for identification. In both situations, the doctor's appearance was the sole factor motivating the man—the real doctor's appearance repelled the man and the fake doctor's appearance motivated him to react favorably.

A far-out example? Not really if it is considered from the standpoint of illustrating the strong impact nonverbal forms of communication have upon others. Indeed, in spite of frequent admonishments to the contrary, we tend to judge people and are motivated, either favorably or unfavorably, by their attitudes, titles, labels, physical appearance, reputations, and even their affiliations. It is therefore important for you to be fully aware of these nonverbal forms of communication and to take advantage of them. Since they can motivate an opponent favorably toward your negotiating objectives, they are true forms of negotiating power.

## THE NEGOTIATOR'S CHARISMA
## AS A SOURCE OF NEGOTIATING POWER

*Power flows to the man who knows how.*

Elbert Hubbard

The way we conduct ourselves unquestionably has a strong impact upon others. We have all heard of the declaration: "He acts like he knows what he's talking about." Or, "I think she's right. I don't know precisely why but I can feel it when I'm around her."

Certain people, by their personal qualities, transmit what amounts to invisible waves. Once these waves touch others, they motivate others as strongly and as persuasively as spoken words.

General George C. Marshall, Chief of Staff of the Army, Secretary of State and Secretary of Defense, was such a person. "The moment General Marshall entered a room, everyone in it felt his presence. It was a striking and communicated force. His figure conveyed intensity, which his voice, low, staccato, and incisive, reinforced. It compelled respect. It spread a sense of authority and of calm."*

Napoleon had a similar impact. Everyone felt his presence the moment he entered a room. His bearing, the manner in which he carried himself, conveyed intensity and compelled respect.

Charisma has nothing to do with having a handsome face or an imposing physique. Napoleon was quite short—less than five foot four. Gandhi was the adored idol of millions not only in British colonial India but throughout the world. Yet his body was thin to the point of emaciation and his face was by no means a thing of beauty. Eleanor Roosevelt, who as a young girl lamented her lack of physical beauty and her crippling sense of shyness, transcended her disabilities to develop a personality and charm that are the very essence of charisma and personal power.

To further illustrate the impact of this type of personal power, consider the following experience. Admittance to a health club requires showing an identification card to a guard at the door. The guard is changed regularly so that there is little opportunity for identification of club members merely by recognition. Yet, there are certain individuals who regularly walk right past the guard without

---

*\*Present at the Creation* by Dean Acheson. New York: Norton, 1969, pp. 141-142.

showing their identification cards. By the way in which they carry themselves they are saying: "I am a member. No need to check my card."

## The Negotiator's Charisma Should Be an Ally

Negotiators' charismas are comprised of a variety of things—the way they stand, sit, walk, talk, gesture and even smile and frown. All of these actions are done in an authoritive manner, automatically without design or calculation. In other words, naturally. This natural manner transmits an air of authority and decisiveness. From the moment an opponent's eyes are on the negotiator, the negotiator's actions should emit that invisible current that motivates the opponent toward the negotiator's side. These actions comprise the whole of how negotiators conduct themselves; how, for example, they walk—a firm, know-where-they're-going type of walk; how they shake hands—a firm, precise handshake that conveys the impression that: "I am pleased to meet you and happy to be able to deal with you on this matter"; how they sit during the negotiation—comfortably firm as if in full command of everything that transpires.

This type of bearing cannot help but enhance the negotiator's negotiating power. The opponent is favorably motivated not only because the negotiator's "I know what I am doing and talking about" manner is attractive but also because the waves transmitted by the negotiator leave the opponent no other alternative.

## Hesitation May Stifle Negotiating Progress

The old adage, "He who hesitates is lost," is aptly suited to negotiation. If the health club member hesitated, no matter how slightly, the chances are very good that the member would not have succeeded in gaining admittance without showing an identification card. The reason is simple. Hesitation reflects lack of confidence and even lack of sincerity. If the negotiator's hesitation is grasped by the opponent, its net effect may be to suddenly shift the negotiating momentum to the opponent. The negotiator's hesitation will make it highly improbable that the opponent will be favorably motivated toward the negotiator's negotiating objectives without the negotiator first regaining the negotiating momentum. Hesitation will cause the negotiator to lose negotiating power.

The moral is that negotiators should hesitate only as a matter of negotiation strategy. Otherwise, they should be unfaltering.

## THE ROLE OF TITLES AND LABELS IN NEGOTIATING POWER

> *In a nation so large and so diverse there are few ways of quantifying intelligence or success or ability, so those few that exist are immediately magnified, titles become particularly important; all Rhodes scholars become brilliant, as all ex-Marines are tough.*
>
> David Halberstam in *The Best and the Brightest*

Titles have been the symbols of power and prestige ever since the human race began. King, queen, earl, duke, sheriff, dean, lawyer, and doctor are some of the titles used to convey power or special competence. Titles can impress. It is therefore a natural and logical extension that titles can play an important role in negotiation.

Actually, titles can be a very powerful motivating factor in negotiation, both from the standpoint of increasing or decreasing negotiating power. They are, however, often overlooked as motivating factors or, if they are recognized as such, are improperly used so that the negotiator does not enjoy their full benefit.

### The Positive Effects of Titles

Important titles such as chairman of the board, president, or dean convey the idea that the persons who have them also have the ability, power, and prestige that go with and are required to obtain such titles. This automatic status afforded a person solely by virtue of a title, if that title is one well thought of by society, provides that person with a source of public power.

This same process that associates ability, power, and prestige with title can be very useful in negotiation. People will tend to think that a negotiator who was capable enough to rise to become chairperson of the board or president or Phi Beta Kappa must therefore be a capable negotiator. That person has gained competence by association in the mind of the opponent. The individual who possesses the title is envisioned by the opponent as having competence in all fields of endeavor, including negotiation, even though the title held may have no direct relationship to negotiation.

This attitude on the part of the negotiator's opponent is precisely what the negotiator should hope for and should do nothing to discourage. In such a situation the negotiator's title acts as a positive motivator and, in many instances, has the effect of making the opponent believe that his or her ability is inferior to the negotiator's ability simply because of the negotiator's title. The opponent's feeling of inferiority will often carry into the negotiation and automatically provide the negotiator with increased negotiating power even before the discussions begin. Whether, of course, the negotiator does, in fact, possess greater negotiation ability than the opponent is another matter. The point is that if the opponent believes the negotiator possesses greater negotiation ability by virtue of the negotiator's title, that belief will be translated into greater negotiation power at the bargaining table—actions follow beliefs and the opponent's actions will be handicapped as a result of these beliefs.

## Do Not Use Titles as a Basis for Judging an Opponent's Ability

Just as an impressive title may cause one to overestimate an opponent's ability, an unimpressive title may cause one to underestimate it. For example, if a corporate president who is negotiating with the general manager of another corporation may tend to underestimate the negotiating talents of the general manager merely because the general manager possesses a lesser title. Yet, the general manager may possess much greater negotiating ability than the corporate president. Nevertheless, the president may slacken his or her preparation and even conduct the negotiation at a level of competence far lower than he or she might employ while negotiating with, say, the president of the general manager's corporation.

## The "Labeling" Factor That Increases Negotiating Power

Whenever I think of the effects of labeling in negotiation, I am reminded of a cagey, small-town lawyer who had the opportunity to negotiate matters with large, established law firms, many of whose members were graduates of outstanding law schools. Almost the first thing the small-town lawyer did was to let his opponents know that he was from a small town and a graduate of a small law school. This, he said, often resulted in his opponents' "letting down their guards" because they equated his negotiating skills with his "small town and small law school" label. His opponents' underestimation of his negotiating skills had the effect of increasing his negotiating power. He knew it, and whenever the opportunity presented itself, he capitalized on it.

Labeling can have an impact similar to that of titles upon an opponent's motivation in negotiation. Members of society have labels, just as they have titles, drummed into them almost from the day they are first able to comprehend. Remember the label "from the other side of the tracks," that signified a low economic and social scale? Or, the "born with a silver spoon in the mouth" label that signified a life of great inherited riches? Whether or not such labels are accurate, people are accustomed to relying upon them and attach to them the attributes and abilities society has envisioned a person with a particular label to possess. So a "small-town" lawyer is viewed as not having abilities equal to those of a "big city" lawyer. Neither is a graduate from a "small law school" viewed as having abilities equal to those of a graduate from a "large, prestigious law school." In reality, of course, labels frequently mislead, and it is not uncommon to find small-town lawyers with as much ability and, in numerous instances, more ability than their big-city colleagues.

**When to Use Titles or Labels in Negotiation**

Any experienced opponent is going to attempt to learn as much about the negotiator as possible *before* the negotiation begins, particularly if the matter to be negotiated is an important one. This detective work ordinarily should disclose any titles or labels that the negotiator possesses. Consequently, it can usually be presumed that the opponent has knowledge of the negotiator's titles and labels and will be influenced by them. It is, however, an error for the negotiator to rely upon such a presumption, even if the negotiator is a well-known individual whose titles and labels are common public knowledge. The opponent may be the one individual who "never heard of" the negotiator. Hence, it is important for the negotiator to see to it that the opponent is fully aware of the negotiator's titles or labels provided, of course, that they are of the kind that the negotiator feels will enhance negotiating prestige and thus negotiating power.

Ordinarily the negotiator should, at the outset of the negotiation, apprise the opponent of any impressive titles or labels that the negotiator possesses. This will not only ensure that the opponent is fully aware of the titles or labels but will influence the opponent as early in the negotiation as possible. The result might be compared to the audience's reaction to two comedians, one of whom is well known and the other a newcomer. The viewing public will normally laugh at the jokes of the well-known comedian as soon as the performance begins even though the jokes may not be particularly funny. The comedian's label as a "star" usually ensures that the audience's response will be favorable. The newcomer, on the other hand, will be held to a much higher joke-telling standard and will have to begin with some really funny lines in order to get laughs. Failure to carry into the performance the label of an established "star" forces upon the newcomer a much greater burden and stricter standard of acceptance than that of the comedian's established counterpart.

**Major Risks of Relying on Titles or Labels**

There are two major obstacles in relying on titles or labels as elements of negotiating power. First, unless an opponent is fully aware of the title or label and what it means, the opponent will not be motivated by the title or label in a manner that is favorable to the negotiator's negotiating objectives. For instance, let's say you, the negotiator, are president of one of the largest manufacturers of drugs, and that you hope to purchase raw materials from your opponent, a potential new supplier. One of the early steps you might take is to tactfully inform your opponent of your presidency and what that means in the way of potential business to the opponent. Once the supplier-opponent fully comprehends this, there is no question that these facts alone will assist to motivate the opponent favorably toward an arrangement with you. Mere title and what it represents thus are converted to negotiating power.

The second major obstacle to relying on titles or labels is that you must be certain that your opponent perceives your title or label as being as important or more important than you do. In the previous example, if the potential supplier had virtually all of the business his or her present plant facilities could handle without costly expansion and was in no mind to undertake such an expansion, the chances are slim that the potential supplier would be materially motivated by the fact that he or she was negotiating with the president of a potentially large customer. Obviously, in such a situation you, the manufacturing president, could be seriously overestimating the power of your title and what it represents. If, on the other hand, you perceived that your title could not be converted into negotiating power, you could choose either to drop it from or underplay it in your negotiating strategy. Or you might seek to persuade the supplier to consider plant expansion and thus "create" a situation in which your title could be converted to negotiating power.

**When You Disclose Your Titles or Labels, Be Careful of Backlash**

When disclosing your titles or labels, you should be careful not to make it appear as if you are setting yourself up as being superior to your opponent. If you do, the opponent may resent the disclosure, and that resentment may make it more difficult for him or her to be truly receptive to your positions. This resentment can result in a loss of your negotiating power.

One of the best ways to apprise an opponent of your titles or labels, and thus substantially reduce the possibility of any opponent backlash, is to make the disclosure as early as possible in the initial introduction. You merely say, for instance, at some point in the introduction, that you are the president of Drug Corporation, one of the largest drug manufacturers in the country. The opponent will normally not be offended by the title or label disclosure when it is done in this manner because most introductions include titles or labels.

## THE POWER OF THE NEGOTIATOR'S APPEARANCE

> *One day Cogia Efendi went to a bridal festival. The masters of the feast, observing his old and coarse apparel, paid him no consideration whatever. The Cogia saw that he had no chance of notice; so . . . he hurried to his house, and, putting on a splendid [fur-trimmed robe], returned to the place of the festival. No sooner had he entered the door when the masters advanced to meet him, and saying "Welcome, Cogia Efendi," with all imaginable honor and reverence placed him at the head of the table . . . .*
> 
> From *Pleasantries of the Cogia Nasr Eddin Efendi*

One of the most obvious yet often overlooked realities in negotiation is that, except for our hands and faces, clothes cover the remaining parts of our bodies in most negotiating situations. There is an old adage, "Clothes make the man." In terms of negotiation, it might be rephrased to "Clothes help make the negotiator."

Research has shown that people base their judgments of another's believability and trustworthiness largely upon the other's appearance which, of course, is materially reflected by the other's dress. Consequently, except when you, the negotiator, deliberately intend to alter your appearance as a matter of negotiation strategy, you should take great care to dress the part of a successful negotiator. Your appearance should "tell" your opponent that you know why you are at the negotiation and that you intend to depart the negotiation with what you came after. What this means in practical terms is that your clothes should fit your individual personality. They should not distract your opponent's concentration from what you are advocating during the negotiation. Loud garish clothes may be in fashion, but if they focus more attention on what you are wearing than on what you are saying or if they fail to enhance your image as a negotiator or force the opponent to draw unwarranted, unfavorable conclusions about your negotiating ability, they should be avoided. You should avoid wearing dark glasses. If you must wear them for medical reasons, you should explain this to your opponent. Dark glasses lend their wearers an air of mystery and may arouse distrust in an opponent. Aristotle Onassis, the Greek shipping tycoon, once stated that his eyes revealed too much of his inner feelings. Therefore he wore dark glasses in order to hide his eyes from his opponents during the numerous negotiations in which he was involved. For him, wearing dark glasses worked, but his was a happy exception. His public image of always wearing dark glasses even helped to make them socially acceptable as part of his standard dress wherever he went and whatever he was engaged in. For the average negotiator and negotiation, however, dark glasses should be avoided.

When you are required to travel, you should carry ample clothing so that you can always have fresh, clean clothes to wear to every negotiating session. It is also important for you to realize that the clothes you wear should fit the negotiating occasion. If, for example, you are negotiating on the golf course, you should wear a golfer's attire. Otherwise, you will appear to be out-of-place and thus lose credibility.

In summation, then, your attire should be considered part and parcel of your negotiating arsenal. You should *consciously* dress to fit the negotiation you are about to engage in and should not haphazardly and ritually don the same clothes with little or no thought concerning their impact upon your opponent. For there is one certainty, an impact they will, indeed, have and hopefully it will be one that positively motivates your opponent toward your negotiating objectives.

## REPUTATION AS A SOURCE OF NEGOTIATING POWER

*A great reputation is a great noise: the more there is made, the farther off it is heard.*

Napoleon

Make no mistake about it. Any time you can carry into a negotiation a strong reputation, you have a definite element of negotiating power. Just as people are impressed by titles, labels, and physical appearance, they are equally influenced by reputations. In most instances, the greater the reputation, the greater the influence.

Napoleon is a very good example of the power that a reputation can wield. He victoriously fought many, many battles, often while heavily outnumbered in both troops and weapons. His prowess as a general was legendary, and entire armies would flee in terror merely at the rumor that Napoleon and his army were approaching. It was estimated that his mere presence on the battlefield was worth between 40,000 to 100,000 troops.

Another good example of the tremendous power that a reputation can exercise is Andrew Carnegie. Carnegie was a skilled businessman with a keen knowledge of people. Competition was beginning to seriously encroach upon Carnegie's businesses and he therefore decided to sell—but at his own price and in his own way. He made a series of public announcements indicating that he was going to fight competition by building new plants and even a new railroad. His competitors, knowing very well Carnegie's reputation as a hard-driving and successful businessman to be reckoned with, began to panic. They sought to put together a combination to buy Carnegie out. An eventual purchase was made. Carnegie's share was in excess of $250 million.

### The Role of the Word "Expert" in Negotiation

If you are known as an "expert," this tends to make your reputation so much the greater. As a result you have stronger influence. Of course, your reputation must be one of substance. If an opponent perceives that you possess a strong reputation and discovers, perhaps even during the negotiation, that your reputation is not well deserved, perhaps because of your performance, the opponent will tend to become more confident. This confidence will increase the opponent's negotiating power and correspondingly decrease your power. Accordingly, the burden is upon you, whenever you have or want the word "expert" attached to yourself, to conduct yourself during the negotiation in a manner that fully justifies attachment of the word "expert" to you.

### Your Reputation Need Not Be in the Field of Negotiation

Irrespective of the area in which you have gained your good reputation, its possession will aid you in negotiation. If, for example, you have a good reputation as a top golfer, it can help influence others wanting to do business with you merely because others will want to be associated with such a renowned golfer. Moreover, an opponent may feel that because you are a top golfer, you must also be a top negotiator, even though that may not be the case. Often opponents never bother to inquire about the negotiating ability of a top golfer (or of anyone else who is tops in a field) but merely make the assumption that the person must be a skillful negotiator by virtue of the prowess the person displays in his or her field.

When you possess a well-known reputation that you feel will influence your opponent favorably toward your negotiating objectives, you should tactfully be certain that your opponent is fully aware of that reputation and perceives it in the same light as you do. And if the opponent first makes mention of your reputation, perhaps at the outset of the negotiation, you should tactfully acknowledge the reputation. This tends to reenforce the opponent's perception of the reputation and is thus more likely to favorably influence the opponent. Often opponents mention a negotiator's reputation simply to satisfy themselves that the reputation does, in fact, belong to the negotiator with whom they are dealing. In other words, they are seeking reassurance.

## ORGANIZATIONAL MEMBERSHIPS AS A SOURCE OF NEGOTIATING POWER

*Character is power; it makes friends, draws patronage and support, and opens a sure way to wealth, honor and happiness.*

J. Howe

Being a member of influential organizations can increase your negotiating power. Membership in certain organizations will confer upon you some of the prestige of the organization itself. Membership in the United States Congress or Senate, membership in a state or the American Bar Association, or membership in a national or local business club or business society can each provide you with additional influence in negotiation. The key is to be certain that the opponent is one who will be impressed by the fact that you are a member of a certain organization and not one who will be "turned off" by it. For instance, an opponent who has had a bad experience with a politician or a lawyer may be affected to such an extent that he or she dislikes all politicians or lawyers. In such an event, obviously disclosure of the fact that you are a current or former member of a political or legal organization will not increase your negotiating power but, in fact, may decrease it. For the most part, however, most opponents will be favorably influenced by your organizational memberships and, normally, the greater the prestige of the organization, the greater will be the influence your membership in it will have on the opponent.

Your negotiating power will be enormously increased if you can learn whether you and your opponent are members of the same organization(s). The sharing of organizational affiliations will tend to promote a warmer and more compatible relationship that will ease the degree of difficulty of the negotiation. The old adage that "Birds of a feather flock together" is, so far as negotiation is concerned, largely correct. It is therefore important that you attempt to determine very early in the negotiation, preferably even prior to the commencement of the negotiation, whether your opponent shares any of your organizational affiliations. If your opponent does, be certain that he or she is aware of this common membership as early in the negotiation as possible.

CHAPTER 27

# Why It Is Necessary to Avoid Large, Initial Concessions

*Knowledge and human power are synonymous.*

Francis Bacon

Negotiators who make large, initial concessions normally come out second best in the negotiation. There is an important reason why. Large, initial concessions swing the negotiating momentum to the opponents, thereby giving them more confidence and making them less likely to make similar concessions of their own. By making large, initial concessions, the negotiator appears in the eyes of the opponents to be holding a weak negotiating position, even if the negotiator's position is, in fact, very strong. The ultimate impact is to lessen considerably the negotiators' negotiating power.

The scenario may go something like this. Assume a landowner wants to sell land that he believes to be worth approximately $1000 to $1500 an acre. A prospective buyer appears and the seller offers to sell the land at $3000 an acre. The buyer, through such means as appraisals and a study of sales of similar parcels of land in the immediate area, establishes a strong case that the land is worth only about $800 to $1000 an acre. The seller, since he really wants to sell, then makes a large concession by dropping the price of the land to $2000 an acre—a one-third price reduction. The net result? The land should go for about $1000 to $1200 an acre. The seller's large, initial concession has placed him on the defensive, and it is a relatively simple matter for the buyer to continue getting concessions until the buyer acquires the land for a very good price.

### How to Avoid Making Large, Initial Concessions

The best way for you to avoid making damagingly large, initial concessions is to be certain, primarily through proper research and preparation, that all of your positions advanced or taken in the negotiation can be substantiated by solid support. If you take this approach, when you meet an opponent who is armed with data to support a much lesser position than the position you have advanced or taken, you can disclose your own supportive material to neutralize your opponent's supportive data.

### What to Do When You Must Make Large, Initial Concessions

Occasionally, even experienced negotiators are forced to make large, initial concessions. When forced into this conceding posture, the important point to remember is to be certain that the concessions do not transfer negotiating momentum to the opponent. The best way to avoid such a loss of momentum is to be certain that the reason for making any large, initial concession is fully explained prior to making it so that there is a realistic basis for making it and the opponent does not gain the impression that it was made because your positions were weak or you lacked confidence in them.

In addition, whenever possible, large, initial concessions should be made on a "something for something" basis. You say, in essence, "OK, I'll concede on this if you will make a correspondingly large concession." Any large, initial concession is thus not a bare concession but one that is traded for a corresponding concession from the opponent and thus the danger of the momentum shifting to the opponent is greatly minimized.

To further illustrate, in the real estate example above, assume the seller of the land, although he initially asks $3000 an acre for the land, discovers that a similar parcel of land next to his land sold for $1500 an acre only one week before. He also knows that his opponent is very likely to be aware of the sale. Therefore he decides to drop the price of his land because he really wants to sell it. He therefore informs the opponent of the sale of the adjoining land and that, as a consequence, he is going to drop the price of his land to $2300 an acre because he still feels that his land is worth that price, explaining to his opponent in detail why he feels that way. This technique has a two-fold effect. First, it establishes a valid reason for the concession so that it doesn't make the seller appear to be dealing with arbitrary values, thus limiting to some extent the transfer of negotiating momentum to his opponent. Second, by disclosing the sale of the adjoining land rather than allowing the opponent to disclose the sale, the seller has played one of the opponent's aces and has thus further prevented the negotiating momentum from swinging decisively to his opponent.

CHAPTER 28

# How Negotiating Obstacles and Difficulties Can Increase Negotiating Power

*Peril is the element in which power is developed.*

W. Mathews

There is a Chinese proverb that says a gem cannot be polished without friction, nor a man perfected without trials. There are several ways you can react to obstacles and difficulties encountered in any negotiation. You can react negatively, perhaps by becoming angry or sullen, or by building up resentment toward your opponent for not cooperating. This approach almost automatically reduces your negotiating power because it prevents you from thinking and acting as positively and constructively as you must if you are going to succeed in making negotiation progress. Your negative attitude will force your opponent to rebel against you and will not motivate your opponent toward your negotiating objectives. Once your opponent rebels, the negotiation's progress comes to a virtual standstill.

Another way you can react to obstacles and difficulties encountered in any negotiation is to remain indifferent. You can pretend that the obstacles and difficulties do not even exist. The problem with this posture is that although it may not necessarily result in an *immediate* loss of negotiating power, it normally results in an *eventual* loss of negotiating power because you fail to develop the experience necessary to deal with obstacles and difficulties that will seek you out in future negotiations almost as certainly as water will seek out the lowest level.

To illustrate how one may encounter obstacles and difficulties, let me draw from an experience that occurred very early in my negotiating career. The issue revolved around whether money transferred from a mother to her children was a gift or a loan. The family representative contended it was a loan. There was no note given by the children to the mother as evidence of a loan nor was any interest paid by the children to the mother. I therefore balked at agreeing that the money was loaned. The family representative became very irate and sought to strew my negotiating path with all sorts of obstacles and difficulties, including threats of litigation. My initial inclination was to agree with the family representative's position in order to escape involvement in any controversy. A further examination of the facts, however, made it seem clear that the money turned over to the children was intended as a gift and not as a loan. I therefore decided to approach the matter head-on. The ensuing negotiations were difficult and, at times, very trying. Eventually, however, the family representative came around to agree with my position.

Soon thereafter I analyzed the negotiation very carefully and realized that the course I had chosen, fortunately, was not only the correct course factually but, just as important, the right course to pursue for essential personal negotiating growth. After the case was over, I became more confident both of my negotiating ability and my ability to confront controversial and difficult negotiating situations, ones that I knew would frequently recur. The reason is simple. Negotiations are carried on between people, and whenever two or more people get together for any reason, there is always the possibility, depending upon the particular circumstances, that obstacles will arise and difficulties will occur.

## You Should Build on Your Ability to Handle Negotiating Obstacles and Difficulties

So I chose the third course, namely, tackling the obstacles and difficulties head-on, as skillfully and as capably as possible. From that point on, I had also set my course for future negotiations. I would not react negatively or passively to obstacles and difficulties encountered, no matter how great they were or how much pressure was involved.

That is the approach that you should endeavor to take. If you work hard and learn to deal skillfully with obstacles and difficulties that crop up during negotiation, you will soon develop a proficiency that will build your negotiating confidence and make you that much more of a forceful, powerful negotiator. Your adeptness in handling obstacles and difficulties will not only impress your opponent but also will force your opponent into a defensive negotiating posture that will make it very difficult for your opponent either to persist with the obstacles and difficulties or to succeed in the negotiation.

# CHAPTER 29

# Avoiding Loss of Negotiating Power by Insulating Oneself from Snap, Often Regrettable, Decisions

*When, against one's will, one is high-pressured into making a hurried decision, the best answer is always "No," because "No" is more easily changed to "Yes," than "Yes" is changed to "No."*

Charles E. Nielson

Certainly it is true that in most negotiations you should approach the negotiation fully prepared to make decisions quickly and decisively whenever you feel the necessity to do so. But what happens in a situation in which you must make decisions in haste and you are not fully prepared to do so or not fully convinced that the decision should be made, or what the correct decision should be?

You may often find yourself in these circumstances because of various reasons such as undue pressure from your opponent, the disclosure of new information, or sudden developments that you had anticipated while making your preparation.

**Action to Take When You Are Unsure of What Decision to Make**

Whenever you are confronted with a situation in which you are in doubt about what decision to make, you should either ask for additional time in order to consider the matter in more detail or, if that is not possible, say no. Often, you will find that your opponent is attempting to deliberately pressure you into making a snap, quick decision, knowing that doing so will make you unable to give due consideration to the correctness of your decision. In order to justify putting the pressure on you for a hurried decision, your opponent may, for example, say that time is of the essence, money can be made if there is no delay in a decision, or someone else (such as another purchaser or seller) will intervene to shut you out.

You should not allow yourself to be pressured by such tactics. Even if you are inclined to say yes on the particular issue being considered but are not absolutely certain, you should, if you don't want to say no, attempt to work out a solution that will give you more time to reflect upon and study the matter.

Assume, for example, that you want to acquire farmland for investment purposes. You hope that the land will appreciate substantially in value in a few years and that you'll then be able to sell it for a nice profit. You find the price of the land fully acceptable. The seller indicates that he or she must have a decision on the land before the day is out. The fact that the land was for sale had been brought to your attention rather hurriedly, and you did not have a real opportunity to fully investigate the land's investment potential although you are fully satisfied that the current asking price is fair. You also have reason to believe that the land would be a good investment. Nevertheless, rather than make a snap decision since land is one of the least liquid of investments, you propose that you be given a ten-day option in exchange for payment of a slightly higher price in the event that you exercise the option to purchase the property. This slightly higher price provides the motivation for the seller to grant you the option. You argue that if you exercise the option, the seller has benefited by the higher price so the seller loses nothing by granting the ten-day option. If the option is not exercised, the seller is still free to sell the land to others after the ten-day option period has expired.

In this manner you have obtained the extra time you need to more thoroughly look into the investment potential of the land. You have thus avoided a snap, hurried decision that could prove harmful. The land, for example, may not be zoned for the right type of development and prospects for obtaining a favorable zoning change are not good. Or the land may be situated next to a nuisance such as a busy airport which may make the property undesirable for family dwelling or even commericial building and you need time to check out the impact of the airport on the property. The point is that there could be a variety of reasons why the land is not as an attractive investment as you originally anticipated and the additional time obtained by the ten-day option may be precisely what you need to be certain that the land is as good an investment as you suspected.

In situations in which the opponent refuses to give the additional time and still pushes for a snap, rushed decision, experience has shown, as previously related, that it was wise to say no because frequently there exists the opportunity to change that no to a yes if a yes later becomes called for, whereas it is not possible in most instances to change that yes to a no.

## Refusing to Say Yes Should Be Distinguished from Indecision

Indecision is contagious and differs sharply from a refusal to make a decision for a valid reason. If you are indecisive, your opponent will quickly sense your indecisiveness and you will dissipate your negotiating power because your opponent will lose respect for your ability and will, in extreme cases, become exasperated with your indecisiveness. This is why it is important that you, whenever you do not want to be pressured into a decision that you may have doubts about, explain to your opponent why you refuse to make the decision or why the decision must be no if the opponent refuses to give you more time to consider and reflect upon the matter. Once a full explanation is given, the opponent may not like it or even agree with it but there is no danger that the opponent will misconstrue your refusal to say yes with indecision and, in most instances, you will find that with a full explanation most opponents will be reasonable and grant the additional time whenever possible.

CHAPTER 30

# How to Deal with Negotiating Mistakes to Minimize Loss of Negotiating Power

*To stumble over the same stone twice is a proverbial disgrace.*
                                                    Chinese proverb

Everyone makes mistakes, including even the most experienced negotiators. Negotiating mistakes usually result in a loss of negotiating power because they act as a brake or they halt any favorable momentum that the opponent has developed toward agreeing to your negotiating objectives. Accordingly, it is important for you to develop a good means of dealing with mistakes so that you can minimize the loss of any negotiating power.

## Learn to Recognize Mistakes Early

Early detection of negotiating mistakes is as important as early detection of fire. Statistics show that the detection of fire during the first few minutes after outbreak is most vital in saving lives and property. Early detection and warning allow early remedial action. Similarly, early detection of crime and the motive for crime increases greatly the chances of early apprehension of the criminal.

The sooner you are aware of a negotiating mistake, the sooner you can take remedial action either to correct the mistake or to acknowledge it and move on with the negotiation.

## Mistakes of Fact

Assume the negotiation involves the sale of a corporation and you have mistakenly advised your opponent that there are one million common shares of stock of the corporation outstanding when, in fact, there are only half as many. If your opponent discovers the error, it will obviously reflect adversely upon your credibility and thus dissipate your negotiating power, since your opponent will not likely be motivated favorably toward your negotiating objectives if he or she feels that you have given erroneous information. This type of factual error can be especially harmful if it occurs late in the negotiation when matters are well along toward a successful conclusion. Obviously, your opponent may become concerned that information you have previously supplied is also inaccurate.

If, on the other hand, you discover your error early in the negotiation and promptly advise the opponent of the error and what the correct factual information actually is, the chances are very good that your credibility will not be damaged and may even be enhanced by the disclosure. In such an event no dissipation of your negotiating power will occur and possibly your power will even be increased. Your *early* disclosure of the error may well enhance your credibility in the eyes of your opponent.

**Errors in Negotiation Strategy or in Use of Negotiation Techniques**

There is always the possiblity that you will err in your negotiation strategy or in your use of negotiating techniques. When you make errors of this type, it is sometimes difficult for your opponent to fully realize that you have erred because only you really know for certain, in the final analysis, the precise strategies and techniques you are using and, hopefully, you are not using them in an obvious manner. But you certainly should know by the results you're getting at the bargaining table. If you employ a certain strategy or technique and find that your opponent's reaction is not as you anticipated, then it should be clear to you that use of the strategy or technique was in error. It is important for you at this juncture to be certain not to continue with use of the strategy or technique and thus compound your mistake. Rather, you should discontinue the strategy or technique as carefully and smoothly as possible, either changing to a new strategy or technique or seeking a recess of adjournment in order to conceive a new strategy or use of new techniques.

Since, as related in Chapter 6, negotiating techniques are the real instruments of negotiating power, their use becomes more specific.

Consequently, it is easier for both the opponent to detect errors in their use and for you to realize that you have erred in using them. Accordingly, it is doubly important that you correct the mistaken use of a technique as soon and as smoothly as possible. Only in this manner can you hope to maintain positive negotiating momentum and to prevent your opponent from detecting, or from attempting to detect, any techniques you use during the remainder of the negotiation. Because once your opponent detects use of a technique, you can be fairly certain that your opponent will be alert to any further techniques you may use.

# CHAPTER 31

# Maintaining Open Options Increases Negotiating Power

*Every man is a volume, if you know how to read him.*
William Ellery Channing

When the late Gamal Abdel Nasser was the leader of Egypt, his relations with the other Arab countries, Western Europe, and the United States were either badly strained or completely severed. When Nasser was unable to obtain any satisfaction from Russia, he had virtually nowhere else to turn for either economic or military assistance. He had narrowed his options down to Russia and when Russia proved unreliable, Nasser was virtually helpless. He had painted himself and his country into a corner.

Back in the feudal days, the leaders of some armies used to cross a bridge and then burn it so that there would be no avenue of retreat for their troops. By so closing their option of retreat, the leaders hoped that their men would fight more feverishly toward victory. Obviously, adopting the same approach in negotiation can lead to catastrophic results when you discover, for one reason or another, that it has become necessary to back away from positions advanced. By "burning bridges," you have effectively lost the option to retreat and thus have dissipated your negotiating power.

**Lawyers, Beware!**

Lawyers are prone to foreclosing their options and thus dissipating their negotiating power. Since they have access to the courts by virtue of their profession, it is not uncommon for them to threaten to

151

## Chapter 31

sue if redress or recovery is not forthcoming on or before a designated deadline. There is nothing wrong with this practice if the matter has been clearly and objectively thought out and the lawyer is fully prepared to proceed legally in the event of no satisfaction on or before the expiration of the deadline. Indeed, as related in Chapter 7, deadline setting is a very effective power negotiating technique that should be a part of every negotiator's negotiating arsenal.

Nevertheless, threats to sue are often made in anger caused by frustration at being unable to obtain a favorable settlement. Or threats to sue may be made by a lawyer who is either inexperienced or who is bluffing. When no satisfaction is forthcoming on or before the deadline, the lawyer is not really prepared to go to court. When no suit materializes, the lawyer has foreclosed negotiating options. Thereafter, the chances of motivating the opponent toward the lawyer's negotiating objectives are, at best, very slim. The lawyer's negotiating power is therefore substantially diminished unless he or she can come up with a genuine reason for again approaching the opponent without the necessity of first filing a lawsuit.

Any skilled and knowledgeable attorney whose client is faced with the alternatiave of either meeting a deadline or being exposed to a lawsuit will carefully and prudently analyze the case and, if the attorney concludes that there is no real basis for a lawsuit, the attorney will experience no real fear. The attorney will therefore conclude that the opponent is threatening a lawsuit out of anger, or inexperience, or bluff, or even that the opponent is lacking in an understanding of the issues involved in the case. Whatever the reasons, not only will the threatening party not obtain any satisfaction but the attorney who is threatened will realize that the opponent, in the event that the opponent fails to file the threatened lawsuit after the deadline has passed, will be substantially reducing his or her negotiating options. Moreover, even if the opponent does file the lawsuit, the threatened lawyer will realize that since there is no real basis for the suit, the opponent has not materially increased negotiating leverage by filing the lawsuit. In addition, once the suit is filed, costs will have to be incurred to defend it and the opponent has thus diminished negotiating leverage by depriving himself or herself from using the incurrence of these additional potential costs as further leverage for reaching a settlement.

The opponent can, of course, still allege that to continue the lawsuit will necessitate greater costs but, for the most part, once a lawsuit is filed, it generally runs its course for a period before any final settlement is reached. Too, the opponent will be incurring similar costs as a result of the lawsuit which tends to decrease the results he or she will be getting at the bargaining table.

**You Should Strive to Eliminate Your Opponent's Options**

When I was a young lawyer just beginning my negotiating career, I was negotiating with an experienced, cagey man who would deftly neutralize any positions I advanced until he had, in essence, practically eliminated all of my options. As my options decreased, so did my negotiating power. I realized I could not hope to motivate him toward my negotiating objectives if I had no suitable positions on which to rely.

This is what you should strive for in every negotiation—to eliminate your opponent's options as skillfully and as quickly as possible in order to enhance your own negotiating power. As your opponent's options decrease, the opponent assumes more and more of a defensive posture and, as we all know, the defense is not the point-scoring arm of any successful team.

This is what happened in Nasser's case. Nasser eliminated his own options. But the Russians allowed him to do so, knowing that Nasser really had nowhere else to go for assistance once his options had been lost. Hence, when Nasser sought to acquire aid from the Russians, he was entirely on the defensive. He could only "ask," not "negotiate." The Russians realized that they possessed all of the bargaining aces and were not about to respond to Nasser without asking for substantial concessions and, even then, Nasser was denied the aid he sought.

CHAPTER 32

# Delegation Can Lessen Negotiating Power

*... there is no knowledge that is not power.*

Jeremy Taylor

As related in Chapter 13, in many negotiations there is more than one negotiating person on either or both negotiating sides. In some instances the negotiation may even be conducted in teams with different persons on each team handling different aspects of the negotiation. A financier, for instance, may handle all of the important financial aspects of the negotiation. A person skilled in planning might discuss logistics such as delivery time and place.

Whenever there is more than one negotiating person on a negotiating side, there is a danger that that side may be yielding negotiating power. Skilled negotiators, in fact, generally like to see more than one negotiator on the opposing side because they know that the chances are very good that a plurality of opponents will increase the opposing side's vulnerability, especially because of the problem caused by delegation of negotiating responsibility and authority. It is true that two heads are better than one but only *if* those heads are able to anticipate and synchronize their thoughts and actions. They must be able to operate harmoniously like the teams of Laurel and Hardy or Fred Astaire and Ginger Rogers. These twosomes were able to blend their thoughts and actions to such an extent that each team literally functioned as if it were an entity. But such teamwork often takes years to perfect. Consequently, since negotiators seldom work together long enough to develop any team skills, there is virtually always some degree of vulnerability when more than one person is negotiating on either of the negotiating sides.

The opposite, of course, is also true. To illustrate, I was negotiating a complex, multi-issued matter that required me to travel to a large, distant city. Upon arriving at the place of negotiating, I encountered four opponents. One sat behind his large desk. The others sat in chairs to his far right. It became clear very early after the discussions commenced that the person behind the desk was going to conduct the negotiations entirely by himself and planned to keep his three colleagues from active participation. Whenever an agreement was reached on an issue, he turned to one or another of the men sitting to his right and gave them instructions on what to do in order to finalize any necessary details. It was also immediately clear, of course, that here was a negotiator who fully understood that delegating authority and responsibility dissipated his negotiating power and, as a consequence, that he was an experienced and knowledgeable negotiator.

**What to Do When It Is Necessary to Delegate Authority**

The two most important points to remember when you must delegate authority are, first, to attempt to control in a precise manner exactly which portions of the negotiation will be handled by each negotiator and, second, to ensure that this strict portioning is religiously observed. If necessary, you should not hesitate to call frequent recesses in the negotiation if any of your delegate negotiators spill over into areas other than those assigned to them.

The primary reason for this stringent approach is to ensure that control over the negotiation will be maintained to a degree that is as great as humanly possible. Loss of control usually results in loss of negotiating power. The converse is also true—the greater the control, the less likelihood of power loss. Actually, in most instances you will find that others negotiating with you will roam into areas of the negotiation not assigned to them. The result is not only confusion among your own negotiating team but also an opportunity for the opponent to capitalize on the confusion.

If the negotiation is important enough and any member of the negotiating team roams into unassigned areas of the negotiation, it may be necessary to replace the erring member.

Finally, it is always well to remember that people, by their very nature, are prone to talking and interjecting themselves into a discussion, especially during a negotiation in which there is often plenty of give and take on both sides. A skillful opponent, in fact, may seek to draw as many of your colleagues into the discussion for a variety of important reasons—to gain important admissions, to learn new facts or to substantiate existing facts, to test the ability of all of the negotiators and even to force you to relinquish control over the negotiations through the confusion that results from allowing everyone to join in the discussion.

# CHAPTER 33

# How Proper Habits Conserve Negotiating Power

*Beware of dissipating your powers: strive constantly to concentrate them.*
Johann Wolfgang von Goethe

Napoleon was able to dictate several letters while writing another, displaying a phenomenal knowledge of the subject matter of each letter as he jumped from letter to letter. But since each letter undoubtedly was about a different subject, Napoleon had to adjust his attention to each as he dictated or wrote. He therefore saved very little time and might as well have dictated or written each letter separately. *Unless an act is habitual,* the mind can concentrate on only one subject at a time. Consequently, it follows that in order for you to keep from draining away your concentration from the important aspects of a negotiation and from thus dissipating your negotiating power, it is essential that you make as many of your personal acts relative to negotiation as habitual as possible so long as the habitual acts do not deprive or draw from your effectiveness at the negotiation.

### Negotiation Acts That Should Be Made Habitual

Your method of preparation should be established and made into a habit as soon as possible. The reason is that preparation normally entails a great deal of time and the sooner you can systematize the way you go about it, the more time you will have for concentrating on developing strategy and the other important aspects of most negotiations. You should also develop an efficient filing system. There is no ideal filing system so you should develop a system that works best for you. You don't want to be distracted from a negotiation by having to search for a file or a document within a file. Locating the file or document within the file should be automatic and should require no more concentration than it takes to comb your hair or to walk. Retrieving filed material should become virtually effortless.

To understand how efficient filing systems can be tremendously beneficial during negotiation, consider the following experience. I was negotiating a very important matter and, after several sessions, I reached a suitable agreement. Just prior to making the final agreement, one of my opponents commented that in a recent speech one of his superiors had indicated that a new court decision had a significant bearing on pending cases dealing with issues similar to those involved in our case. He therefore suggested that we might hold off making a final agreement until my opponents had an opportunity to determine whether the new court decision would affect our case. Fortunately, I had read the speech and had a copy of it with me at the negotiation. Because of my efficient filing system and the habit I had developed of retrieving material swiftly, I was able to reach into my briefcase and produce my copy of the speech at virtually the same time I was pointing out to my opponents that the speaker, their superior, had made it clear in his speech that the new case would not apply to existing issues such as those in our case. I pointed out the exact part of the speech in which that comment was made. With this reassurance that they were not finalizing an agreement that was contrary to their superior's position, my opponents made a final agreement immediately. My habit of maintaining an efficient file thus became my ally and prevented me from dissipating my negotiating power on a matter of great importance.

## Other Good Habits That Can Increase Your Negotiating Power

Everything in your office or place of work should have a proper place and be in its place so that virtually no concentration is required to locate it instantly.

There are other good habits that can be developed. For example, if you are required to travel frequently, you should systematize as many of the traveling aspects as possible in order to free your mind for concentration on the negotiation. This means that your luggage should be packed in virtually the same manner each time with each item of clothing allotted a certain spot. You should develop surefire and simplified routines for obtaining transportation and hotel accommodations.

Have you ever, during your travels, seen someone rummaging through pockets looking for an airplane ticket? That is a sure way to dissipate one's power. The better way is to always keep the ticket in the same place so that it can be found automatically.

Your personal habits, so long as they are good habits and work for you, should extend to such basic things as where you keep your car keys, handkerchief, and money. These may seem like little things but, just as they do in most other aspects of life, little things mean a lot in negotiation and can, indeed, often mean the difference between success or failure.

Finally, it is significant to note the impact habitual acts can have upon an opponent. In the experience above, when I was able to effortlessly reach into my briefcase and pull out a copy of the speech at a second's notice, my actions obviously conveyed to my opponents the message that I was well prepared and schooled in the subject matter of the negotiation. Even more importantly, my opponents were virtually shut off from making further arguments because of my quick response that put them on the defensive and, in essence, indicated that their further thoughts about any other aspects of the negotiation would be met with similar responses. In other words, by acting promptly I was able to reassure my opponents that they could conclude the negotiation without worrying that they might have done something to displease their superior.

CHAPTER 34

# The Necessity to Avoid Succumbing to Negotiating Pressures

*Nothing gives one person so much advantage over another as to remain cool and unruffled under all circumstances.*

Thomas Jefferson

One thing is almost as certain as rainwater is wet and sunshine is warm—the longer one negotiates, the greater are the chances that one will become engaged in a negotiation in which there will be an opportunity to become ruffled. In professional sports, the phenomenon is frequently referred to as "choking."

I recall one vivid instance in which a professional golfer had to make what ordinarily should have been an easy two-foot putt on the last hole of a highly prestigious tournament. He needed the putt to win. If he missed it, his opponent, who had already finished his game, would have a tie. Thousands of fans crowded around the eighteenth green watching. All the television cameras were focused on him. There was a dead silence. The pressure was simply too great. He became ruffled and putted the ball right by the cup. This goof gave his opponent the tie, and a playoff became necessary. The golfer who choked lost the playoff, too.

### The Harmful Consequences of Becoming Ruffled in Negotiation

In the situation just discussed, the opportunity to win the tournament was entirely within the control of the golfer who was confronted with the two-foot putt. All he had to do was to push the ball barely 24 inches—two feet—and the victory was his. Once he missed, his opponent not only tied him but also gained considerable momentum that carried the opponent forward in the playoff to win the tournament.

The same chances of becoming ruffled or of "choking" are present in negotiation. By becoming ruffled at any point in the negotiation, especially at critical points, you may provide your opponent with an opportunity to retain a commanding negotiating position and, equally as important, to gain the negotiating momentum. Once this occurs, your opponent has a decided edge in the negotiation from that point on unless you are somehow able to reverse the process.

An additional harmful consequence is that once you set this pattern into your way of thinking and reacting, you will be more likely to become ruffled in subsequent negotiations. This will be true whether the negotiation is large or small and even whether it is simple or complex. For when your mind is presented with the same or similar circumstances that previously forced you to become ruffled, you will, again, react in the same manner.

The same is true of the professional golfer in our anecdote. If he doesn't work hard to develop stability and discipline, he will choke in virtually every situation in which he is on the eighteenth (or final) hole, faced by thousands of fans and television cameras, and his final putt means the difference between winning or tying or losing. For some athletes, getting ruffled has resulted in premature termination of what have been promising professional careers. Getting ruffled can have the same devastating results in negotiation.

**Ways to Prevent Becoming Ruffled or Choking**

There are several methods to assist you to keep from becoming ruffled or choking. I use the word "assist" because, in the final analysis, the only sure way to tip the scales in favor of remaining cool and unruffled in all circumstances and, therefore, gaining a considerable advantage, is through discipline and rigid determination not to succumb to the numerous pressures that surround you as you engage in negotiations.

One good way to avoid becoming ruffled or choking is to be certain that you are soundly and completely prepared for the negotiation. Sound and complete preparation not only provides you with confidence as you enter into the negotiation but also provides you with confidence as the negotiation progresses and you discover that you are really better prepared than your opponent is. A confident person will not choke or become ruffled because confidence is the very opposite of choking or becoming ruffled.

Another good method to use to avoid becoming ruffled is to develop the ability to remain cool and confident in as many negotiating situations as possible so that your mind is trained to react coolly and firmly throughout each and every one. This method of gaining experience is really important because each experience that is handled coolly and firmly will reinforce the type of healthy reaction that will enable you to remain cool and firm when faced with potentially ruffling situations.

Finally, another good way to assist in avoiding becoming ruffled is to utilize the mental practice in the manner previously explained in Chapter 22. By mentally conceiving all of the situations in an up-and-coming negotiation that may present themselves as ruffling situations and coolly and firmly dealing with them mentally as explained in Chapter 22, you will be primed to handle those situations very effectively when or if they actually occur.

To take a simple, everyday occurrence, assume the negotiation involves the return of a defective product to a discount store. Before ever going to the store, if the disgruntled customer visualizes the entire sequence of events of returning the product and getting a refund, including the potential dialogue that may occur with the store's representative, and mentally deals effectively with any objections raised by the store's representative, the chances are very good that the entire negotiation will run smoothly with no ruffling even if the going gets rough.

CHAPTER 35

# Abuse of Negotiating Power

*There is nothing that people bear more impatiently, or forgive less, than contempt: and an injury is much sooner forgotten than an insult.*
                                                                Lord Chesterfield

You should set and strive to attain definite negotiating objectives. In doing so you should not set out to annihilate your opponent. An opponent who feels that he or she has been treated harshly or has been badly beaten will, sooner or later, attempt to even the score. It is, therefore, wise to approach any negotiation as if you will, on some future occasion, negotiate with the same opponent. Frequently, in numerous cases you will.

The ideal situation, and the one that you should strive for, is to attain your negotiating objectives, at the same time leaving your opponent feeling good about the outcome—perhaps even feeling like a winner. But there is a great difference between feeling like a winner and being a winner and if you have accomplished your negotiating objectives in conjunction with leaving your opponent in a good state of mind about the outcome of the negotiation, you have truly succeeded.

To illustrate, a client invested money in a business venture on the basis of certain representations. The representations did not prove to be accurate and the client desired to get his money back without going through a long and costly court action. In seeking to accomplish this objective, two positions were taken at the negotiation: one, that the representations had been inaccurate, and two, that there existed no authority on the part of the opponent, a corporation, to enter into the transaction because the transaction did not comply with the opponent's corporate charter. Violation of its corporate charter greatly concerned the corporate officers of the opponent because it exposed them to possible stockholders' liability.

After several negotiating sessions it was agreed that the invested money would be returned and the issue of violation of the company charter would not be pursued. Hence, the final outcome pleased the opponent even though the opponent was required to pay back the invested money.

You should always bear in mind that even if you never negotiate with the same opponent again, you may be negotiating with that opponent's close friend or business associate or acquaintance. If you annihilate your opponent, you can be sure that the chances are very good that your opponent will not speak highly of you if the opponent learns that you are negotiating with the opponent's friend, business associate, or acquaintance. In such an event, your road to negotiating success with any of these other individuals can only be more difficult. Contrast that to a situation in which your opponent has departed the negotiation feeling good about the outcome and even, perhaps, feeling like a winner. His report to his friend, business associate, or acquaintance will, in such a case, undoubtedly be favorable to you and can only serve to help you build up considerable negotiating goodwill and thus increase your negotiating power.

**What to Do When There Has Been an Abuse of Negotiating Power**

When Abraham Lincoln was running for the Presidency, J. S. Moulton, an influential Chicago man, looked upon Lincoln's candidacy as something of a joke and was very unfriendly toward him. After Lincoln won the election, he attended a reception at one of the Chicago hotels. Moulton was in line waiting to pay his respects to Lincoln but had entered the line only as a formality. When his turn came to greet Lincoln, Lincoln said, "You don't belong in that line, Moulton. You belong here by me." Everyone at the reception witnessed the honor bestowed upon Moulton and from that time on Moulton became one of Lincoln's strong friends and supporters.

Lincoln's story vividly illustrates the impact of transforming an enemy into a friend merely by a genuine act of kindness. Lincoln's act said in essence, "Look Moulton, the past is past. I have a very high regard for you and I want you to be my friend. You and I should work together." Moulton, of course, responded. How could he resist?

It has been said that if you desire to make a dangerous man a friend, ask him to do you a favor. This technique, although it should be practiced with great caution, can help to convert a disgruntled opponent into a happier one provided, of course, that the request for a favor is genuine.

## There Is No Set Amount of Negotiating Power to Use in Any Given Negotiation

The amount of negotiating power to be used in any negotiation is only that amount that is necessary for you to accomplish your negotiating objectives. To go beyond that point is to risk abusing negotiating power and may result in harmful consequences.

There is no formula for you to apply to determine when you have reached the point of the desirable amount of negotiating power to use in any negotiating situation. Rather, an accurate negotiating power cutoff point can be determined only by applying your experience with emphasis on your knowledge of people and especially on your knowledge of the particular opponent involved in the negotiation.

It is impossible to overemphasize the necessity and benefits of postnegotiation analysis in order to determine not only whether negotiating power has been applied properly but also whether too little or too much negotiating power was applied. Religiously adhering to both experience and postnegotiation analysis should soon bear fruit. And as you continue to gain experience, you should be in a position to determine with a great degree of accuracy the proper amount of negotiating power to apply in any given negotiating situation.